D1479591

ABORIGINAL AUSTRALIANS
SPIRIT OF ARNHEM LAND

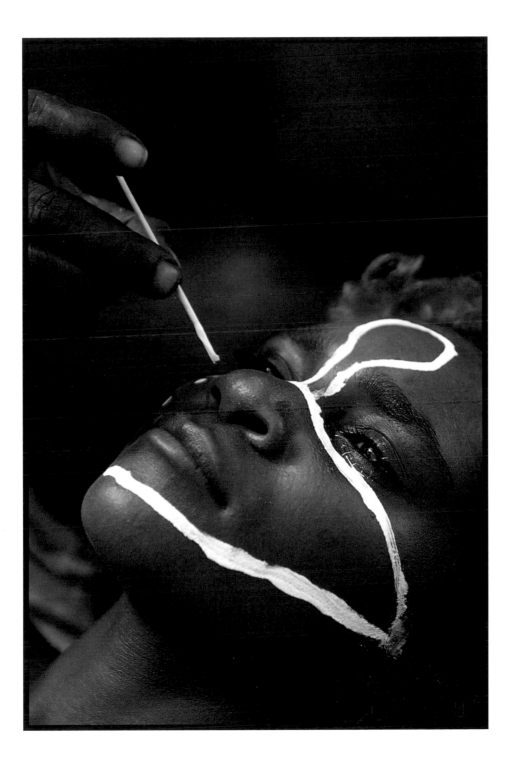

NEW HOLLAND

Ŋarra buku-gurrupan nhumalany
warrpam'nha dhiyak djorraw'djämaw.
Djambarrpuyngu

Manjbun duninj bu kanbidyikarrmeng.
Kunwinjku

To Ben

In the past Aboriginal people deemed it inappropriate to mention the name of a deceased person for a certain period of time. This practice is still current in many places. In some communities seeing a photograph of the deceased could also cause distress.

Before undertaking this book every family in Arnhem Land with whom I worked was consulted about this matter. Everyone generously agreed that I could include certain photographs and names of relatives who had passed away. They also agreed that if a family member was to pass away any recent photograph could still be included in the book. They told me: 'We want our people to be remembered, we want our young people to know about their ancestors and remember their deceased relatives.'

Nonetheless, I should warn Aboriginal people that in this book there are a few photographs of people who have passed away. I apologise for any distress this may cause their extended family, and hope they understand that these photographs are included because it is the wish of close relatives to honour their memory.

Penny Tweedie

ABORIGINAL AUSTRALIANS
SPIRIT OF ARNHEM LAND

PENNY TWEEDIE

It was an important part of this project that the Aboriginal people with whom I had worked could see and approve this material; so before publication I took the proof pages back to Arnhem Land. This last essential consultative process was made possible by the generous assistance of the Rio Tinto Aboriginal Foundation. The book met with much interest – 'Yo Manymak!', 'Gamarrk!' – and everyone's approval. The generous friendship, cooperation and advice of the Aboriginal people involved had made it possible to capture a glimpse of the spirit of the people themselves, their culture and their country – the spirit of Arnhem Land.

There are over sixty languages spoken in Arnhem Land. Each language has a commonly accepted standard orthography, or spelling style. Words that are common to more than one language may therefore be spelt differently depending on the orthography of the language in question. Where possible, the Aboriginal language words in this text are spelt using the respective standard orthographies currently accepted by the various Arnhem Land language groups.

Where possible every Aboriginal person included in the book has been named, using both the English and Aboriginal names for adults and the English names only for children.

Penny Tweedie

Contents

PREFACE

In 1975 I left one desert assignment with the nomads in the Sahara for another in Central Australia, flying to Alice Springs to photograph the filming of *Bourke and Wills* for the BBC. It turned out to be an experience that changed the direction of my life.

Sitting one day in a creekbed with several of the Aboriginal cast, who were waiting to film, one of the elders (now deceased) began drawing patterns with his hand in the sand. As I watched he talked about the caterpillar, his ancestor Yippirinya, who travelled through the country like a human. As he mapped out swirls and lines he said, 'You take picture of this, show those whitefellas. Our spirit is in this land, this land she's like our mother.'

Over the next few weeks this elder would occasionally command my attention with a silent gesture to show me something, a plant that was good to eat or a place he wanted to talk about, always proudly instructing me: 'You take picture, you show your people.' His desire to share this knowledge intrigued me. I started asking questions and haven't really stopped since.

In August that year the Gurindji people of Wattie Creek, about 600 kilometres south of Darwin, were granted 3250 square kilometres of land on Wave Hill Station – the first successful claim to traditional Aboriginal land. I photographed the memorable moment when Prime Minister Gough Whitlam scooped up a handful of dirt from the ground and slowly poured it into the hands of Gurindji elder Vincent Lingiari. In being a witness to this historic turning point for Aboriginal rights and future claims to their lands, I was inspired to continue working with Aboriginal people to help tell their story.

Photography can be intrusive and also exploitative, but it can provide valid visual documentation if the objective is clearly understood. I had already worked in more than fifty countries with other ethnic groups and tribal peoples, and I was acutely aware that proper discussion and agreement between the photographer and the people being photographed is an essential part of the process.

In 1978 David Malangi, a well-known artist (whose bark painting had been reproduced on the original Australian one-dollar note), arranged for me to visit and work with him and his family at Yathalamarra, his outstation near Ramingining in central Arnhem Land, approximately 475 kilometres east of Darwin. By this time, I had an eighteen-month-old son, Ben, and was accompanied by his father and a childminder. I was apprehensive that the Yolngu families (people of central and eastern Arnhem Land) we camped with would find us too much of an intrusion. But the curiosity of having a white toddler in their camp proved a novel attraction, and our campfire became a focal point for discussion and much merriment.

After a few weeks several of the elders at Ramingining decided to incorporate us into their social structure by giving us appropriate skin names. In Arnhem Land every Aboriginal person belongs to one of two groups, or moieties, either Dhuwa or Yirritja (spelt Duwa and Yirridjdja in some areas). The moieties are divided into four categories making a total of eight skin names, male and female. This system of kinship establishes a detailed blueprint for everyone's relations and relationships. Each relationship has its own accepted obligations, responsibilities and customs of behaviour.

I was informed that I was Yirritja moiety and that my skin name was to be Bulandjan. I realised with dismay that I had been named skin sister to two of the artists with whom I was working – George Milpurrurru and Johnny Bungawuy (now deceased), who were both Bulany, my brothers. In Arnhem Land the brother–sister relationship is supportive but forbids physical, verbal or eye contact.

Balandika turns my camera on his mates.

I tentatively asked how we were going to be able to go on working together. There was an interminable silence before they all laughed and said it was okay because I was only a skin sister and I was Balanda (whitefella) anyway. This new status meant that I was automatically related to every individual in Arnhem Land, whether as sister, mother, daughter, mother-in-law, aunt or grandmother.

Over the ensuing months all the people we encountered were extremely proud of their culture and wanted it recorded, not just for themselves but to show and share with us whitefellas. Responding to their curiosity to see my photographs, I held a slide show under the stars at Ramingining to show the work in progress, and within days received invitations to work with many other families.

Whether hunting, gathering or just sitting around the camp, we were led gently and unsuspectingly into the intricate knowledge they have of their environment. Every facet of the surroundings had another level of meaning. There weren't just plants or rocks; these things had their uses, they had a story. Specific places would be pointed out: 'That's where the quoll was living, that one I told you had an argument with the moon.' And they would embark on telling us (as if it were only yesterday) about the spirit ancestors who, during their adventures at the beginning of time, had created the world and all its creatures.

I came to learn that everything, past and present, is somehow interrelated. The stories of the ancestors, the complex social structure and the law are all interwoven in time and space with the land from which they stem. This law is kept alive through the Aborignal people's elaborate cycles of songs and ceremonies, and through their art.

In 1979 I was able to assist with arranging for David Malangi, George Milpurrurru and Johnny Bungawuy to exhibit their work in the Sydney Biennale at the Art Gallery of New South Wales. This exhibition was a landmark for Aboriginal art, acknowledged for the first time as contemporary art by international critics. This was the artists' first experience of a big city and we camped together in a flat in the suburb of Balmain. Seeing our crazy consumer society through their eyes was a revelation that posed many questions about our own culture and caused much hilarity. From here I returned to Arnhem Land to finish the work for my first book, named by David Malangi *This My Country*.

My work as a photographer then took me on assignments around the world with many remarkable people, but the inexplicable link I felt with Arnhem Land remained. In 1995 I returned to Ramingining community to discuss the idea of undertaking another book. Their enthusiastic welcome was only flawed by the joking reproach I received from them for not bringing Ben back with me.

Since the 1970s a lot of things have changed. Aboriginal politics, land rights, the stolen generations (Aboriginal children taken from their families and integrated into white Australia) and reconciliation are now mainstream issues. At a local level the power base has shifted: local councils run their own communities, with the missions (once the spearhead of government policy on Aboriginal affairs) providing back-up expertise. Bark huts and bough shelters have been replaced by basic housing, microwave technology has now brought communication to the remotest areas and solar panels provide power to isolated outstations. Clinics, schools and consumer goods abound but, at the family level, not a lot has changed. Terry Yumbulul at Galiwinku explained: 'We are managing our own communities. Some Balanda work with us to help with business, but we are the bosses now.'

In Arnhem Land Aboriginal lifestyle retains its traditional roots. Hunting, gathering and ceremony business continue with vigour. The people are determined to ensure their children 'learn the proper way' and that Western values don't undermine their efforts to keep the culture strong and the sacred knowledge intact.

As David Malangi explained further: 'I'm talking to the young people, telling them about our ancestors, explaining them our country, how to hunt and find bush tucker and making ceremony to pass on the law.' It was in this context that the idea for this book was approved and developed, not just for a Balanda audience but as elder, David Karlbuma, from Korlobidahdah, said: 'We want this book for our people, so we can show our grandchildren and they can show their children.' And so the project took off.

ACKNOWLEDGEMENTS

A book of photographs accompanied by the words of the Aboriginal people portrayed would not have been possible without weaving together enthusiasm, support and cooperation from many different sources. Especially important was the keen participation of many Aboriginal people in Arnhem Land.

In 1995 the Australian Institute of Aboriginal and Torres Strait Islander Studies (AIATSIS) supported my idea, and their invaluable research grant made it possible to get started. AIATSIS looks after a unique visual archive on indigenous Australians, which is kept on their behalf. For twenty years I have donated photographs to this collection in the knowledge that these images will always be available to the Aboriginal people whom I photographed.

My very special thanks go to Dr Stephen Wild at AIATSIS and to Tamsin Donaldson; to Dr Nicolas Peterson at the Australian National

Ramingining kids hitch a ride with Ben.

University for his checking of the final manuscript; to my editor Kerry Davies; to Dorothy Bennett, intrepid expert on bark paintings, for encouragement and advice; to linguists Murray Garde, Dr Melanie Wilkinson and Steve Etherington; and to botanist Pina Guiliani at the Museum and Art Gallery of the Northern Territory.

Once in Arnhem Land the Aboriginal families I hadn't seen for years welcomed me back. I made new friends and, with everyone's help, guidance and good humour, this book evolved. My most sincere thanks go to all the families with whom I camped and worked, went hunting, got bogged and sheltered from the storm; who welcomed me into their family life and offered me this glimpse into their lives, while instructing me in the spirit of their culture and their country.

I especially thank respected elder of the Liyagalawumirri clan David Malangi, and my ngapippi (skin uncle), who was the first to take me under his wing, and whose extensive family has taught me so much; George Milpurrurru, my wawa (skin brother), magnificent artist, much feared clan leader and renowned medicine man, who cured my son Ben of a serious fever when he was only two; David Karlbuma, Tom Noytuna and Jackie Bunkarniyal, who welcomed me back to Korlobidahdah like an old friend; Jimmy Njiminjuma, his brother John Mawurndjul and their families; Mick Kubarkku and his family; the family of the late Johnny Bungawuy; Linda Wulamana and family; Bunduk and Dhuwarrwarr Marika in Yirrkala; and Terry Yumbulul and Clely at Galiwinku, Elcho Island.

Thank you to the Injalak artists and the traditional owners at Kunbarllanjnja (Oenpelli) who introduced me to their country, which sings with spirits both past and present. And thank you to everyone at the outstations of Nangalala, Yathalamarra, Yikarrakkal, Mumeka, Kakodbebuldi, Malnyangarnak, Korlobidahdah, Galawdjappin and Dippirri, where I learnt new bush skills and how to survive with mosquitoes, leeches and hungry dogs. And a special thank you to everyone at Ramingining community and surrounding outstations. You have all patiently put up with my coming and going over the years and you probably haven't seen the last of me yet!

Mobility was the essence of these expeditions and without Land Rover's generosity it would have been impossible. Their latest four-wheel drive Discovery had to contend with every type of terrain from rock climbing to river crossings via the ubiquitous Arnhem Land swamps and, despite many boggings, never let me down.

Hanimex Fuji's support for this project in supplying film has been invaluable and CPL Services in Melbourne generously sponsored the excellent processing of it. To be photographing for months on end, sending film for processing but not being able to see the result is a photographer's nightmare, but occasional calls from bush telephones to Darren at CPL provided vital feedback.

I would also like to thank the following companies whose generous contributions assisted this project: Ansett, Psion, Qantas, Canon, Vision Graphics and Ward Air.

Without 'Two Moore Miles' in Kakadu this project could have got seriously bogged in bulldust and black swamps, but Jane Moore and Greg Miles never failed to raise my flagging spirits with wisdom, humour and encouragement. I also want to thank all my friends in Darwin who made a home for me and all my 'baggage', especially Ken and Carol Conway, Pam and Peter Garton, Richard and Patsy Creswick. And in Sydney, Phil Quirk and Grenville Turner at Wildlight for their help and professional advice, and to Brian Williams and Deborah Wrightson for their insight and patience.

And a special thank you to my long-suffering family and friends, especially my mother, in England, who has never complained about my commitment to photography and its demands, and always remembers to prune the roses for me.

TRACING THE HISTORY, FORGING THE FUTURE

'Today, we Aboriginal people of Arnhem Land are responsible for our land. We control our future and our destiny, as we did for tens of thousands of years before the Europeans came. But it hasn't always been like this, since the arrival of the first foreigners we Aboriginal people have had to fight for our survival, our culture and our rights.'

Gatjil Djerrkura OAM, Arnhem Land elder;
Chairman, Aboriginal and Torres Strait Islander Commission

AN ANCIENT PLACE AND PEOPLE

As told by George Chaloupka OAM, D.Litt. (Hon.), FAHA, Curator Emeritus, Rock Art, History and Culture Unit, Museum and Art Gallery of the Northern Territory

Arnhem Land is a special place of outstanding natural beauty. An area of around 97,000 square kilometres, it extends from the sweeping beaches and islands of the Northern Territory's north-eastern coast, through mangrove swamps and serpentine estuaries, past freshwater wetlands and eucalypt woodlands to weathered sandstone plateaus with their sculpted cliffs and gorges filled with relict rainforests.

Although this was one of the first parts of the Australian continent sighted by Europeans, it was one of the last regions to be subjected to the vagaries of 'progress' – a place where Aboriginal people had lived relatively undisturbed until the turn of the twentieth century. Along with its unique beauty and remoteness, it is a region rich in resources: food, water, bush medicines and materials that amply supply all the people's requirements.

Aboriginal people use the expression 'the land is my mother' to describe their intimate relationship with their physical environment and all the living things within it. They say that they have always lived here, ever since the beginning of time, when the female ancestors and those who followed them, the first people, formed their land, created animals and plants, placed conception spirits in their waterholes, gave them their language and their law, and taught them religious practices to ensure the regeneration and wellbeing of all species.

These ancestral beings also taught them living skills, such as how to make and use weapons and implements and how to live in harmony with the land. Some of these beings were human, or at least partly human; others are known to have changed from human to animal form or vice versa. They remain in the landscape and in Aboriginal oral traditions as Dreamings, living legends that tell of the experiences of these creation ancestors.

Aboriginal people believe that Arnhem Land's distinctive landmarks and natural environment exist in their present forms as a result of the creation ancestors' activities and what they left behind. Billabongs and rivers, rock formations, rainforests, springs and plains, like the paintings and engravings on the walls and ceilings of rock shelters, are evidence to local people that the stories are true.

The pattern of living set by the creation ancestors is passed on from generation to generation through binding social relationships. In the social structuring of their universe, Aboriginal people divide everything that exists in their world into two categories known as moieties. Within this system, the people, the land, and the animals and plants are specifically and intimately related, and it is through these links that the sacred past is drawn into the present – the sacredness of the land being fundamental to the understanding of life.

Aboriginal art testifies to this intimate link between the people and the land from which they come. Its significance lies in its use as a timeless vehicle for recounting the history and retelling the ancient stories to each new generation.

HISTORY REVEALED THROUGH ROCK ART

As told by George Chaloupka

Archaeological excavations of two painted rock shelters in Kakadu National Park, which borders Arnhem Land to the west, indicate that people first settled this area over 50,000 years ago. From that time on, they painted with ochre pigments in order to satisfy their need for expression and decoration. In these and thousands of other sites across Arnhem Land's vast sandstone plateau, lies Australia's greatest cultural heritage: the rock art of the Aboriginal people – evidence of the world's longest continuing art tradition and home of the world's largest collection of rock paintings.

From soon after the time they first settled this continent up to the present, Aboriginal artists have recorded in vivid paintings their view of their ever-changing physical, social and spiritual environment. With the onset and end of the ice ages, sea levels rose and fell over time, as did average temperature and rainfall, affecting the availability, distribution and existence of animal and plant species.

In order to cope with these changes, the early Aboriginal people developed suitable weapons and implements, adopted new hunting strategies and introduced into their art and oral traditions the stories of the ancestral beings in explanation of the forces surrounding them. The art that is preserved in their painted rock shelters collectively forms an encyclopaedia of their human experience and endeavour, providing an invaluable legacy of their history.

The ancestors of present-day Aboriginal people are thought to have reached Australia during the low sea levels of the most recent ice age. They moved from one protective shelter to another, leaving on the rock surfaces marks of their presence: hand stencils – paint sprayed

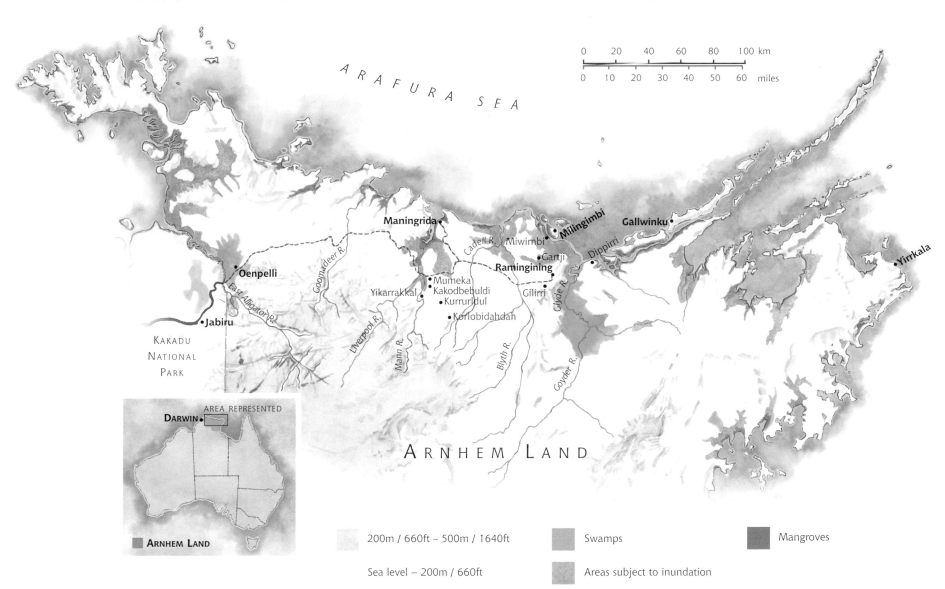

from artists' mouths – and imprints of their palms. Their later more figurative paintings tell us that men of this period used boomerangs and multibarbed spears to hunt kangaroos on the open plains, agile wallabies along the river banks, and rock wallaroos, possums and large pythons in the escarpments. Women, portrayed with digging sticks and string bags, gathered vegetables and hunted small animals.

Early artists also depicted the large animals that were to become extinct over the closing stages of the ice age. There are paintings of single-toed kangaroos that are much larger than present-day species; a representation of a tapir-like diprotodontoid that browsed on the foliage of shrubs and trees; a marsupial lion that stalked its prey through the woodlands; and depictions of the long-beaked echidna that rummaged through the humus of escarpment rainforests. These and subsequent generations of artists also recorded the presence of thylacines (Tasmanian tigers) and Tasmanian devils, until these species were displaced by the introduced dingo.

Now superimposed by layers of colourful paintings of more recent times, most of the early, weathered rock art – rendered in red ochre – is said to have been executed by the ancestral Mimih people. This belief is supported by the location of some paintings in places now inaccessible due to weathering and other geological forces – evidence to the Aboriginal people that they were painted by the Mimih, who had the power to move rocks at will. Mimih taught the predecessors of today's Arnhem Landers how to paint, and the tall and slender spirits who live between the rocks of the escarpment – the kin of the ancestral Mimih – continue to visit some of the local artists in their dreams and suggest to them what they should paint.

Over many thousands of years, artists depicted animal and human subjects in various distinctive styles, from complex figurative images sketched with the finest of brushes, to front-facing static silhouettes, and later to one-line-thick stick figures. Each style depicts the figures with their complex apparel and many items of their rich culture. Males carry boomerangs, spears and, later, a hooked stick originally used as a fighting pick that evolved into a prototype spearthrower, or woomera. The boomerangs were often stencilled onto the rock surface, documenting their actual dimensions and shape. The figures wear an assortment of elaborate headdresses, pubic aprons and bustles,

necklets, pendants, tassels, armlets and leg ornaments. The women, without adornment, are depicted with dilly bags, digging sticks and occasionally with a stone hatchet. Humans, animals and creatures of the imagination were arranged by artists into narrative compositions depicting hunting, fighting and ceremonial scenes.

The most enigmatic rock-art images of all are representations that are based on the outward form of yams, with their raised nodules, stylised rootlets and vines. Over time these simple paintings developed into human, animal and imaginary creatures. The best known of these entities is the Rainbow Serpent, depicted as a composite being with a kangaroo-like head, a snake's body, and a serrated tail based on that of a crocodile, or a palm frond.

It was during this period, about 6000 years ago, that the sea was reaching its present level, flooding the river estuaries and introducing into the local environment a number of new fish species as well as the saltwater crocodile. These creatures were at first depicted in a quite naturalistic manner, but the later X-ray renditions, where animals and humans are shown with their bone structure and internal organs, became dominant. Some of the region's most beautiful paintings were executed in this stylistic form, which has become the best known of all Arnhem Land art forms and continues to be used to this day. Later again, and also in the X-ray style, are the first paintings to portray men playing the didjeridu.

Among more recent paintings are depictions of subjects associated with the Macassans and the arrival of the Europeans. This rock-art period began some 300 years ago when fleets of Macassan vessels arrived each December with the north-west monsoon from the islands of what is now Indonesia . They would spend several months along the coast of Arnhem Land gathering and curing trepang, otherwise known as bêche-de-mer or sea-cucumber, before returning home with the south-east trade winds in March or April. During their extended period of contact, the Macassans established close social and economic ties with the coastal groups, and had considerable influence on the art, myth, ritual and material culture of the wider Arnhem Land region. Paintings of the Macassans' distinctive praus, with the hulls containing dugout canoes, bags of rice, bamboo containers and woks, feature in this period of rock art.

Mandarrk's Rainbow Serpent at Dukaladjarranj.

Barramundi in X-ray style and female and male figures at Nanguluwarr.

Figures at Nourlangie Rock.

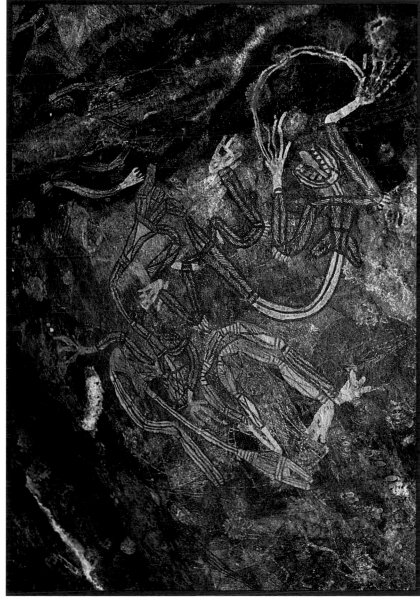

Male and female Namarakin spirits at Sorcery Rock.

Painting by Jimmy Njiminjuma showing cross-hatching (rarrk).

Hollow log story by Andrew Margululu.

Frilled lizards by Andrew Margululu.

Crocodile by George Milpurrurru

European contact with the north is also well documented in Arnhem Land's rock-art record. There are paintings of sailing boats, steamers, men bearing arms, introduced animals, dwellings, buffalo shooters, missionaries, a bicycle, a motor vehicle, guns showing bullets in the breech, in addition to aircraft and letters of the alphabet. Detailed compositions depict exploration parties, the overlanding of cattle, the building of the Pine Creek railway, Darwin's wharf in the 1890s and, more recently, a passenger plane, of the sort that would have passed through Darwin on its way to London in the early 1950s.

A number of well-known rock artists were still practising their skills into the 1960s. In 1964 Nayombolmi (known to many as Barramundi Charlie), Djimongurr and Djorlom filled the Anbangbang shelter at Nourlangie Rock, one of the best known of the Kakadu art sites, with brilliant new paintings. A year later Mandarrk, later renowned for his works on bark, executed a 4.5-metre representation of a Rainbow Serpent on the ceiling of the Dukaladjarranj shelter in Arnhem Land.

Rock painting was not the only art form practised in Arnhem Land. Throughout the years, people painted or carved on bark sheets, artifacts and ceremonial poles. It is, in fact, on these mediums that the art of the people of Arnhem Land continues into the present.

CONTINUING HISTORY AND TRADITION THROUGH BARK PAINTING

As told by Penny Tweedie and Dorothy Bennett, Aboriginal art consultant

In the vast areas of Arnhem Land where there were no rocky overhangs for shelter, Aboriginal dwellings consisted of bark sheets over wooden frames. Some groups in the 'stone country' also preferred these bark shelters, especially after earth tremors had caused rock overhangs to collapse. As with rock shelters, people painted on the inside of these dwellings. These paintings were not intended for permanence, and the bark panels were abandoned to perish from exposure or bushfires as people moved from place to place with the changing seasons.

In Arnhem Land, elaborate bark paintings were first recorded in the early 19th century. However, Europeans showed little interest in bark painting until Baldwin Spencer, Chief Protector of Aborigines, arrived in Arnhem Land in 1912. While at Kunbarllanjnja (Oenpelli), Spencer was so impressed by the art that he began to collect bark paintings,

even commissioning works himself and paying for them according to size with sticks of tobacco (to this day the Aboriginal people of Arnhem Land still refer to cigarettes as 'sticks'). Spencer later donated these works to the Museum of Victoria in Melbourne.

Bark paintings were created not only for pleasure but also to instruct the younger generation in spiritual beliefs and ceremonial business. Since the hundreds of languages spoken by the Aboriginal tribes of Australia were not written, painting was an important means of communication, in addition to song and ceremony, by which to pass on information and the law.

Some bark paintings, for use in ceremonies, were made to last. Complex and elaborate paintings with purely symbolic designs were, and in some cases still are, kept with other sacred emblems and regalia in sacred storehouses – such as caves and special shelters – and brought out and used exclusively during certain ceremonies. Paintings were also used as a means to evoke fear and sorcery – a warning to people to keep the law and abide by its rules and taboos.

Some paintings have many layers of meaning and contain symbolic designs that have specific meaning to the initiated, in addition to the figurative image. These symbols are also painted on the bodies of young initiates, and on burial poles and on hollow logs for mortuary rites. On such occasions they can be seen by others, but their real meaning is only known to those who are fully initiated. As David Malangi, elder of the Liyagalawumirri clan, explained when painting Milmildjarrk, his sacred waterhole: 'It's okay you see this painting, this is my waterhole, made by one of the Djangkawu sisters. I can tell you this, but this painting also has secret-sacred story I cannot tell you. I teach my sons this story, paint it on them for their initiation and we sing and dance this story in our ceremony … This is how we keep our culture strong, pass on this sacred story.'

David also explained the tough and time-consuming process of making a bark painting: 'First we got to find the right stringybark tree [a type of eucalyptus], straight and strong, no knots, no cracks… First we cut around the tree, one cut at the bottom of the good piece, then cut a forked pole to climb up, cut at the top; then cut from top to bottom and peel the bark from the tree. Only cut bark in wet season, no good cutting in dry season because that bark is too stiff, will crack.'

All loose external bark is then scraped off the piece and its surface is smoothed (shark skin was used before the advent of sandpaper). The cylindrical bark is held over the hot ashes of a fire to flatten it, and then laid on the ground, weighted down with large rocks, and left to season for several days. To further prevent the bark from curling, sometimes the top and bottom are strapped to thin branches with bush string made from stringybark.

The most critical part of any painting, whether on bodies or on bark, is finding good colour. The traditional colours of red, yellow, white and black are still used in most areas of Arnhem Land. Red and yellow ochre are found in many rocky outcrops across the region; good charcoal from fires is plentiful and provides the black; but white is hard to find, whether as white pipeclay from rivers or chalk found in rocky outcrops in the stone country.

A slab of rock serves for a palette into which colour is ground and mixed with a little water to form a liquid paint. The juice of an orchid stem was once added to create the fixative, now standard wood glue is used. Brushes are made from fine strips of bark frayed and softened at the end, and certain grasses chewed to a fine point. To create the rarrk – the fine cross-hatching so characteristic of Arnhem Land art – artists use a piece of pliable palm leaf or a few strands of human hair attached to a twig. The artist first applies the background colour – of red or black – then outlines the main design. The detail is usually built up layer upon layer, with the cross-hatching painted last.

By the late 1980s these distinctive bark paintings were in high demand from dealers, galleries and collectors internationally. It was around this time that foreign collectors introduced the artists to good quality paper and canvas, both more enduring and more portable than bark and available at any time of the year. Now many artists paint on paper occasionally and some works on paper have been specially commissioned. But bark is still used widely, especially in central and eastern Arnhem Land.

In Arnhem Land, despite the introduction of new mediums, the art continues to reflect its cultural heritage. As George Milpurrurru, ceremonial leader of the Ganalbingu clan explained: 'My father Ngulmarmar and my uncle Luluna [both deceased] taught me to paint, showed me, told me the stories I can paint, the story about my ancestors, my totems, my country. But I don't copy what my father did. I paint my way. Things just come in my head, how to paint, how to paint that story. Painting is hard job, to cut good barks, find good colour, need very steady hand and always thinking … like being inside that painting … Sometimes my painting has many stories. I am boss for Gumang, magpie goose … My painting is about my country, about my Dreaming. I painting my law so it can last forever.'

AN ENDURING LAND, PEOPLE AND CULTURE

As told by Penny Tweedie, with comments by Gatjil Djerrkura taken from the author's interview with him in October 1997

Arnhem Land, by its very isolation, has remained relatively protected from the influence and often devastating impact European settlement had upon Aboriginal people in other parts of Australia. In Arnhem Land, the traditions, the customs, rituals and beliefs, and the ways of living that allowed the Aboriginal people to survive on this continent, are still apparent after 50,000 years.

Yet development has had an impact. Dutch seafarers landed on the coast of Arnhem Land during the early 1600s, when they charted Australia's northern coastline from Cape York in the east to Carnarvon in the west. Soon after, the Macassans began their seasonal trepang industry, bringing economic and cultural exchange. In the 1800s the British, who had claimed and colonised the east of the continent, began to look to the north.

Throughout the 1820s and 1830s three military settlements were established in the Top End and soon abandoned as isolation, cyclones and disease took their toll. Relations with the local Aboriginal people were mixed, dependent on the practices of individual commandants. There were killings on both sides at the first two settlements, Fort Dundas and Fort Wellington. But at Victoria, on the Cobourg Peninsula, the Aboriginal people, used to contact with the Macassans, helped with the construction of the settlement.

Further land exploration and surveys led to a permanent settlement at Port Darwin in 1869, paving the way for the cattle industy and gold mining. There was a rapid increase of the predominately male non-Aboriginal population, leading to liaisons with, and exploitation of, Aboriginal women. Many settlers found it hard to cope with the harsh

Jazmin being painted for his initiation ceremony at Yathalamarra, 1997.

Richard Birrin Birrin with his son Jazmin painted for his initiation ceremony.

conditions and tropical climate, so Chinese and other Asian immigrants were recruited into the labour force. They also introduced opium use. The Aboriginal people's way of life changed dramatically in the face of the advancing colonial frontier.

'In those days cattle was the only industry in northern Australia,' explains Gatjil Djerrkura. 'The cattle men came up from the south and the Yolngu found themselves having to interact with each other much more. Until then it was taboo for one clan to enter another clan's country unless they were invited. But the coming of the white man's cattle industry changed that and people had to move.'

But in Arnhem Land the cattle industry did not take hold. The north was unsuitable country for cattle, and any attempts to stock large leases in eastern Arnhem Land were thwarted by poor conditions and Aboriginal attacks on cattle. The pastoralists responded with systematic massacres, but the people resisted and the cattle companies pulled out. 'In Arnhem Land people weren't forced off their land as happened in other parts of Australia,' says Gatjil.

Yet the coming of the pastoralists was a real threat to the life and livelihood of the Arnhem Landers. Pastoralists and Aboriginal people fell into a pattern of killings and reprisals that became common throughout the Northern Territory, as it was elsewhere in Australia. It was partly for this reason that Christian missions moved into the Territory: to provide protection for the Aboriginal people, to prevent further loss of land, life and dignity.

'In those early days the Church played a very important part in providing protection from the slaughter and the government policies that occurred in other places,' says Gatjil. But he adds: 'The mission people and those white men [government administrators] thought they knew what was best for Aboriginal people ... they deliberately stopped some of our cultural practices.'

The Church Missionary Society established the first Arnhem Land mission at Roper River, on the southern border of Arnhem Land, in 1907. Others soon followed. The first missionaries banned ceremonial life and the sacred rituals, and recruited the people to work in the vegetable gardens, build houses and make roads, for which they were rewarded with weekly hand-outs of flour, tea and sugar, and the much-prized tobacco. Children were segregated into dormitories, and thus

protected from what were considered the 'undesirable aspects' of tribal life, though not all missions endorsed the practice.

The Commonwealth Government assumed legal guardianship of Aboriginal people in 1911, controlling every aspect of their lives. In 1913, Aboriginal reserves were set aside across the Territory, including Arnhem Land, for which permission was required to enter or leave. From about 1911, part-Aboriginal children were taken from their mothers and installed in institutions in Darwin and Katherine, and later on Groote Eylandt and Croker Island. Gatjil points out that in this 'the Church played its part as an agent for the government'. The Aboriginal victims of this policy, which continued to some degree until the early 1970s, are now known as the stolen generations.

The Arnhem Land missions, the last of which was established in 1952, were to change much of the Aboriginal way of life, but they also brought some benefits. As Gatjil says of Yirrkala mission, which operated from 1935: 'Aboriginal people were drawn to the mission to stay. The Church provided food and work, and people were attracted by the clinic. It changed our culture from survival in the bush, people could stop in one place.'

The advent of World War II brought about further changes. The northern coastline became Australia's first line of defence against the Japanese. Part-Aboriginal children were taken interstate and a number of Aboriginal people were moved into supervised camps, many to work on the army farms, hostels and hospitals, as well as in active service. Arnhem Land communities provided a ready coast watch. 'Some of our people were involved during that period,' Gatjil recalls. 'People were taken by the military forces. No one can say we didn't play our part in protecting this country of ours. Aboriginal people were messengers, observers of coastal areas and some were recruited into the services. Some of them were never seen again.'

By 1944 more than 1000 Aboriginal people were involved in the war effort, earning five shillings a week plus full rations, medical care and accommodation. The relatively equal treatment of Aboriginal and white Australians in the military created an interaction in the following decades that led to a new set of expectations by Aboriginal people.

Meanwhile, the discovery of minerals in Arnhem Land from the 1950s posed a new threat to its people. Although Arnhem Land was a recognised Aboriginal reserve, the Crown retained the mineral rights. In 1963, when the Commonwealth Government leased 330 square kilometres of tribal land around Yirrkala to the Swiss mining company Nabalco, the people of Yirrkala petitioned Parliament with two bark paintings inscribed in Gumatj: 'Give us back our land. If you take away our land you take away our soul.' Gatjil says: 'By this act the people of Yirrkala gave birth to the land rights struggle in this country'. 'We were the first indigenous people to stand up for our rights and to challenge the doctrine of terra nullius.' In 1970, they took their case to the Northern Territory Supreme Court. Although the court ruled against the claim, the case opened the debate for land rights.

Throughout the 1970s the impact of white settlement upon the rights of the Aboriginal people continued as an increasing number of mining companies ranged throughout Arnhem Land prospecting for minerals. In Arnhem Land the mining companies built townships for thousands of non-Aboriginal workers, creating new tensions. 'That's when our people really began to be affected by these industries,' Gatjil recalls. 'We had an additional challenge – to live with another law and culture, to try and adapt to another society, but at the same time to try and maintain our own culture and traditions.'

Aboriginal people became increasingly distressed as the intruders wantonly ignored advice, invaded areas of Aboriginal significance and damaged sacred sites. 'This led Aboriginal people to say enough is enough, and to want some of the benefits from the mining of our land,' says Gatjil. 'That's when Aboriginal people became more vocal.'

In 1976 the Aboriginal Land Rights (Northern Territory) Act was passed and the people of Arnhem Land were granted inalienable freehold title to their land. But living in the various Church missions and government settlements restricted people to living side by side with their extended families. Cramped into small areas with rival clans, this situation was beginning to create friction and unrest. And having to deal with two legal systems – Balanda law and Aboriginal law – added to people's confusion and discomfort. The difficulty of trying to maintain Aboriginal custom amid the increasing social problems prompted a few of the elders to go back to their clan country and set up camp: these became known as 'outstations'. Others soon followed and the outstation, or homelands, movement was born.

'The outstation movement is the only hope that I see to stop the trend in family breakdown, and the breakdown of law and order,' says Gatjil. 'The social issues worry me, social issues in terms of Western culture versus Aboriginal culture. We are seeing a lack of respect for the old ways and a lack of attendance at ceremonies. People are breaking the traditional law to escape into the white man's culture. Living on an outstation provides reassurance of one's identity and also one's cultural credibility.

'People are going home [to their land] to find their links. Leaders are reasserting their traditional authority. Young people who move to an outstation with their family find more respect and find role models. There is a strong sense of direction and responsibility.'

During the 1980s and 1990s mining royalties brought prosperity, training and jobs to some areas of Arnhem Land. Self-determination and self-management were welcomed, but required new skills and responsibilities. While material goods, modern communications and the latest technology have catapulted even the remotest outstations into the twentieth century, it has also at times created a conflict of culture, particulary among the younger generation.

'There is a lack of interest among young people that we need to change,' says Gatjil. 'If self-determination and self-management are to be achieved, then we need to take control of our own destiny. In my opinion, we need to control the infrastructure, with government assistance. Things like education, health, training and employment need to be taken over by Aboriginal people. Unless we can do this we will never achieve true self-management.'

In Arnhem Land, victories have been achieved, while old struggles continue to be dealt with and new challenges faced. 'Arnhem Land is still a paradise, it is still in the hands of its original owners,' says Gatjil. 'We Arnhem Landers are taking our future into our own hands. We must get more involved, we must exercise our traditional authority. We need to do more to make both systems [Aboriginal and Balanda] work for the future of our people, our children and our culture. In other parts of Australia the culture has been lost, but while we are isolated we are confident of holding onto our own. The land is our mother and Aboriginal people have to stand up and be counted to protect our motherland.'

Mishak, Matthew and Jeremiah playing sticks and didjeridu at Dukaladjarranj.

Growing up in Arnhem Land

The personal life history of David Malangi as told to Penny Tweedie.
David lives in his mother's country at Yathalamarra. Language: Djinang. Clan:
Liyagalawumirri, Manyarrngu lineage. Moiety: Dhuwa, subsection Gamarrang.

David Daymirringu Malangi was born in 1927 in his father's country at Maliyana, on the eastern side of the Glyde River. David's family, including two brothers and four sisters, lived in bark huts or under bough shades, moving through their clan country according to the seasons and the best hunting. In the wet season, they stayed in his father's country, an area of beautiful billabongs that rises up from the flood plain. In the dry season, as the Arafura swamp slowly dried out, their hunting grounds extended into his mother's country, Yathalamarra, on the western side of the river, towards Milingimbi. David says that they were '… always walking about, forwards and backwards in our country. My father, my mother, our family always walking about, sometimes just for hunting, sometimes old people making ceremony, taking that ceremony to other people.'

They had no possessions or clothing apart from the spears and fishing nets that they made, a stone axe and, later, a steel-head axe. When they needed shelter they made bough shades and platforms to sit and sleep on, and in the wet season they roofed these with strips of stringybark. Under the platforms they lit small fires on which they piled leaves to smoulder and deter mosquitoes. At night they covered themselves with paperbark to keep warm.

Recollecting his earliest memories, David says, 'I'm thinking, first thing I been thinking about is that bunggul.' (A bunggul is a genre of song and dance.) David saw a white person for the first time when he was 'maybe seven, maybe nine'. He chuckles at the memory. 'Asking my father: "What's this? Maybe something wrong with that one?" My father said: "That's Balanda, that one white man." My father told me those old people thought they were seeing the spirit of someone who had passed away.' Many Yolngu were frightened of the white man but, as David says: 'My father said he was missionary, not bad person.'

He remembers how he was taken to school at Milingimbi: 'My father, he left me at the school.' He remembers crying because there were so many kids and lots of teasing. 'Miss Watson gave me material and made me wear naga [loincloth]. I'd never worn any clothes before.'

School was held under a tree and the children were given their own chalk and a board to write on. When I ask David what he learned, he says with a laugh: 'Not much!' and starts mimicking a child's best schoolroom sing-song: 'One, two three, four … A, B, C, D.' 'Miss Watson was strict,' he says. 'But she was kind and gave us food.' He stayed several months at school, but never learned to read or write.

As a young man he worked for a while with the mission's cattle at Milingimbi. First he had to learn to ride a horse, so one of the experienced Yolngu stockmen showed David what to do while the Balanda boss watched and shouted instructions. He became a good rider and enjoyed the job, learning to train new horses and crack a whip. He laughs as he describes the trials of learning to milk cows. David worked as a stockman for several years. At the time, Aboriginal stockmen were paid about five shillings a week and given basic rations of flour, tea, sugar and tobacco.

David was at Milingimbi during World War II and clearly remembers planes flying low over the settlement. He describes in detail seeing the bellies of the planes opening up and spewing out their bombs, while he was running away to hide in the mangroves. 'Too much planes, too much noise and hurting people with those bombs.'

At Milingimbi, David also helped build the stockyards, worked on the farm and even took his turn at being 'police boy' for the vegetable garden. When the men weren't working they went hunting for wallaby, goanna, magpie goose, turtle, fish, crab and occasionally for crocodile. 'That one hard job,' he grins, 'when everyone hungry for fruit'.

After his initiation into men's business – young men are initiated into traditional law through a series of ceremonies and initiation rites – his parents arranged his marriage to Elsie Ganbada. Later he took three more arranged wives, Rosie Wutam, Judy Baypungala and Margaret Gindjimirri. Today they all live together at Yathalamarra with ever-fluctuating numbers of their extended family.

David started painting as a young boy, taught by his father and his uncle to paint on bodies for ceremonies, on hollow logs for burials and, later, on stringybark. He was taught to paint the story of his creation ancestor, Gurrumurringu, the story of the Djangkawu sisters. He painted the stories that they sang about in their ceremonies, and his totems the sea eagle, crow, snake and goanna.

It was while thinking about how to paint the complicated story from the Manharnju ceremony that David created the complex bark painting that made him famous. This painting was represented on the Australian one-dollar note, initally without his knowledge. When the then Governor of the Reserve Bank, the late Nugget Coombs, became aware of this he awarded David with a medal cast in bronze and an aluminium boat. The ensuing publicity assured a market for his bark paintings. David's art is now in collections in Australia and abroad, and has taken him to Australia's State capitals, New York and Tahiti.

David's life today contains many of the trappings of modern living: a house with electricity, a television and video player, a refrigerator, a leather attaché case in which he locks his precious items, and one smart city suit. But he still lives predominantly on the ground, sleeping outside under a mosquito net, huddled beside the embers of a fire with most of the older members of his household.

He paints in the breezeway between the rooms of the house, sitting cross-legged on a blanket and jockeying for space amid his family's activities, a game of cards, a wife kneading damper, another weaving pandanus, numerous children, people trying to sleep and a dozen dogs scrounging for scraps. Although he admits that many things are much easier now than when he was growing up, David points out: 'Today too many worries, too much argue for money, for cars, wrong skin marriage, too many new worries.'

David is particularly concerned to keep his culture strong, to ensure the survival of the Yolngu tradition: 'I'm talking to the young people, telling them about my family, telling them about the ancestors, the story of this country, and making bunggul to teach them singing for our country and our story. We make bunggul to bring everyone together, men and women, so they know the true story.'

It is six o'clock in the evening, and as we talk a group of children and teenagers have gathered in front of a Christian cross, three metres high and painted white. They start to practise line dancing, to the accompaniment of American religious tape-recordings on their ghetto-blaster, in preparation for fellowship. David raises his eyebrows, then yells at them to turn the volume down.

'Sometimes I worry about the young people, not caring for our culture, all the time listening to Balanda music, making fellowship business, drinking kava, too tired for hunting, not listening to the old people … Like Yolngu medicine and Balanda medicine, both good medicine … Fellowship business has good story for our community. Maybe they can learn God's message, and Yolngu business too.'

On 19 April 1996 David Malangi was awarded a Doctorate of Laws by the Australian National University in Canberra for his 'distinguished creative contribution in the service of society'. The certificate David received that day honours him with the words: 'David Malangi, senior artist and elder statesman of the Manyarrngu people, who through his artistry has communicated the values and aspirations of Aboriginal people and thereby assisted all Australians to understand and benefit from the culture of his people.'

David in the billabong at Yathalamarra.

Events of significance

c. 60,000 years ago Ice Age, Aboriginal people reach Australia

c. 20,000 years ago Use of edge-ground tools

c. 6000 years ago Present sea level attained

1606–44 Dutch make sightings of northern coast, and chart coastline. Willem Van Colster in the *Arnheim* first to land and name Arnhem Land, 1623

c.1650 Macassan (Indonesian) trepang industry begins on Arnhem Land coast

1699 British exploration of west coast

1770 Captain James Cook charts east coast, claims British possession

1788 Colony of New South Wales established, under principle of terra nullius (literally 'land belonging to no one'); subsequent estimates place Aboriginal population at 500,000

1802–3 British chart Gulf of Carpentaria

1817–21 British chart northern coast

1824–29 Fort Dundas, Melville Island, established and abandoned

1827–29 Fort Wellington, Cobourg Peninsula, established and abandoned

1838–49 Settlement of Victoria at Port Essington, Cobourg Peninsula

1844–62 Overland expeditions explore the north, including parts of Arnhem Land

1863 Northern Territory of South Australia declared

1864–66 Settlement of Palmerston at Escape Cliffs, mouth of Adelaide River

1869 Palmerston (later Darwin) established at Port Darwin

1872 Overland Telegraph Line, Adelaide to Palmerston, completed; gold discovered at Pine Creek, south of Darwin; first cattle brought to the NT

1881 First Darwin census records population of 3451 (670 European, 2781 Chinese or part-Aboriginal – Aboriginal people of full descent not counted)

1885 Government Resident reports on killings, disease, prostitution and use of opium among Aboriginal people; recommends setting up reserves

1901 White Australia policy implemented – repatriation of Chinese, ban on further migration

1907 Church Missionary Society (CMS) establishes mission at Roper River – segregation of children in dormitories

1910 Aborigines Act passed in SA Parliament, giving legal sanction to confinement of Aboriginal or part-Aboriginal people in reserves or institutions

1911	Commonwealth takes over the NT; Aboriginal Ordinance gives Chief Protector of Aborigines legal guardianship of all Aboriginal people and part-Aboriginal children. Children taken to compounds in Darwin and Katherine – first of the 'stolen generations'
1912	Baldwin Spencer appointed Chief Protector
1913	Spencer reports on 'wholesale prostitution of Aboriginal women and ... supplying of opium and spirits ... especially in mining districts'; recommends segregation through reserves for Aboriginal people of full descent, compounds for town dwellers; Aboriginal Ordinance makes police responsible for control and protection of Aboriginal people
1914	World War I – Spencer's proposals shelved
1916	Methodist mission on Goulburn Island, later at Milingimbi (1923), Yirrkala (1935), Galiwinku (1942)
1918	Spencer's earlier recommendations reintroduced through new Aboriginal Ordinance
1924	CMS sets up centre for part-Aboriginal children from the mainland on Groote Eylandt
1925	Oenpelli, former government pastoral lease, taken over by CMS
1927–29	Bleakley Inquiry proposes use of missions in 'segregating, protecting, training and control of the Aborigines' on behalf of Government
1931	Arnhem Land declared Aboriginal Reserve
1938	Umbakumba flying boat base established, Groote Eylandt
1939	New Deal policy for improving conditions for Aborigines announced, not implemented due to outbreak of World War II
1941	Methodists set up centre for part-Aboriginal children from the mainland on Croker Island
1942–45	Japanese enter World War II, air raids on Darwin; part-Aboriginal children taken to SA and NSW
1946	New Deal policy implemented, opening the way for Aboriginal settlements (Umbakumba 1946, Maningrida 1957, Ramingining 1966)
1951	Manganese found on Groote Eylandt. Commonwealth–State conference agrees to policy of assimilation
1952	CMS mission at Numbulwar
1953	Bauxite found near Yirrkala. Welfare Ordinance passed, making Aboriginal people of full descent wards of the State, granting full citizenship to part-Aboriginal people (implemented 1957)
1962	Aboriginal people granted Commonwealth and NT voting rights

1963	Government resumes 330 sq. km around Yirrkala, leased to mining company Nabalco; people of Yirrkala petition Parliament with bark painting demonstrating ownership
1965	BHP (Broken Hill Proprietary Co. Ltd) begins mining manganese on Groote Eylandt, building town for 1500 white employees
1966	Court grants award wages to Aboriginal stockmen, defers implementation to 1968. Gurindji clan stockmen and families stop work at Wave Hill Station, south-west of Katherine, set up camp at Wattie Creek, petitioning the Governor-General to secure tenure
1967	Referendum amends Constitution to enable Commonwealth to make national laws for Aboriginal people and include them in national census
1968	Nabalco begins mining bauxite on Gove Peninsula, builds town of Nhulunbuy for 5000 white workers within 20 km of Yirrkala
1969	Uranium found in western Arnhem Land
1971	Yirrkala case against Nabalco, challenging terra nullius, lost in Northern Territory Supreme Court
1972	Labor Party wins government pledging policy for self-determination – Dept of Aboriginal Affairs established; Woodward Land Rights Royal Commission; Fox Inquiry into uranium mining
1975	First legally recognised Aboriginal lease granted to the Gurindji people
1976	Aboriginal Land Rights (NT) Act passed by new Coalition government; people of Arnhem Land granted inalienable freehold title; Northern Land Council (NLC) formally recognised to negotiate over mining and royalties, represent traditional owners in land claims and manage areas granted
1977	6000 sq. km adjacent to Arnhem Land granted to Kakadu Aboriginal Land Trust, leased back to Commonwealth for Kakadu National Park (declared 1978). Coalition announces decision to proceed with uranium mining in Kakadu
1978–80	Uranium mined at Narbalek; Ranger uranium mine opens 1980; township of Jabiru built
1982	Kava introduced to Arnhem Land by Uniting Church as substitute for alcohol
1990	Aboriginal and Torres Strait Islander Commission (ATSIC) set up
1992	Mabo judgment overturns terra nullius, acknowledging Aboriginal prior ownership
1996	Wik judgment opens Native Title claims; claim over Croker Island and surrounding waters, known as Wik of the Seas
1997	Release of *Bringing Them Home*, report of the stolen generation inquiry

LAND

The Aboriginal people of Arnhem Land believe that the creation ancestors, or ancestral beings, emerged with the dawn of time and travelled across a dark and empty land creating the landscape, water, sea, stars, wind and every living thing. These creation ancestors were sometimes animal, and other times human, and could metamorphose into spirits, rocks or any thing. As they travelled across the land the ancestral beings created the land formations, gave birth to the people, named their clans, and created the plants and animals on which to survive.

On their travels, the creation ancestors met with other beings from different clans. Sometimes these beings were good, sometimes dangerous or evil. Through their interactions, these creation ancestors established the basis for social organisation and laid down Aboriginal law. This law and kinship system has guided Aboriginal society for thousands of years. It is celebrated in song, dance and ritual; it is also portrayed in rock art and bark painting.

Aboriginal people have been living in Arnhem Land for more than 50,000 years. The ceremonies celebrating their religious or totemic rites are not less than the title deeds to their clan country. From a rock shelter at Dukaladjarranj, David Karlbuma of the Barabba clan looked out across the billabong below toward the eucalypt and acacia bushland that shimmered to the horizon. David explained the responsibility he has to his clan's country: 'We are the custodians for this country. Our ancestors looked after this country, they told us the stories about the creation of this land, its rocks, waterholes, trees and creatures; about the creation spirits who made our people and our law. Our elders taught us this, sang and danced these stories, painted them on rock shelters. We pass on this law to our children just as our ancestors did for us, in bunggul (a genre of singing and dancing) and ceremony. We tell our children these stories so they will tell their children, who will tell their children, on and on forever.'

Contemporary Aboriginal people are linked to the creation time through their totems, which join individuals to the natural world around them. The Aboriginal people of Arnhem Land know their totemic ancestors and sing the songs associated with their clan's history, or Dreaming. In recounting these stories, or singing their Dreaming, Aboriginal people ensure the continuation of these beliefs and their relationship with the land.

As Thompson Yulidjirri explained while pointing to a cave of layered paintings near Injalak: 'This is like history. We are part of this land and this land is part of our being.' In 1971, during the Yirrkala land rights case, Galarrwuy Yunupingu explained to the Northern Territory Supreme Court in Darwin: 'My land is mine only because I came in spirit from that land, and so did my ancestors of the same land … without land I am nothing.'

Long time ago this was a dark and empty land. Then the sun travelled across the land spreading warmth and light. The creation ancestors made this land, made the rocks, waterholes, trees and creatures. They made the people and our law. Aboriginal people are part of this Dreaming. We came from this land, it is part of us. We are custodians for this land and our law.

Donald Gumurdul and Bill Namundja

Bill (opposite) is the tour guide at Injalak, an important rock-art site in western Arnhem Land. Children (above) at Yikarrakkal paint up for fun and to ward off evil spirits.

Coming back to our country, to our rock shelters, caves and waterholes makes everyone feel good. Maybe we catch fish, gather tucker, just being in our own country makes us feel strong. We bring our children and tell them the stories of these special places. In Arnhem Land, everyone knows the stories for their own country. The stories are our link with our past. This is what we tell our children when we go into our country.

Jacob Nayinggul and David Karlbuma

Jacob's nephews Thomas, Brian and Rowen (above, left to right) play the didjeridu and clap sticks at Wulk in western Arnhem Land. Two hundred kilometres further east at Dukaladjarranj, David's son Jeremiah (opposite, at right) and nephews Matthew, left, and Rowen paint up with pipeclay.

I am traditional owner for this place, Injalak. My grandparents lived in these rock shelters. I bring my sons Nathan and Vincent here to show them these paintings so they will know this place, know the stories of our ancestors. Some of these paintings are very old, thousands of years old. Maybe those ancestors painted on the rock while waiting for rain to stop. Maybe they were telling story about hunting or the Mimih spirits. So many paintings, sometimes one on top of another.

Donald Gurmurdul

Donald, Vincent and Nathan (opposite, left to right) at Injalak, an important site for the Kunwinjku people. Rock painting (above) in Anbangbang shelter at Nourlangie Rock, Kakadu National Park.

We are custodians for this place called Dukaladjarranj, that means place of the possum. Long long time ago the Rainbow Serpent, Ngalyod, travelled across this empty land making rocks, waterholes, billabongs, all things. At Dukaladjarranj Ngalyod was thirsty, so she made a sweet billabong. This made her tired, she needed to rest, so she spat out these rocks to make a shelter. My uncle, David Karlbuma, told me this story.

Mico Rostrin

Jeremiah (opposite and above, at left) and Mico (above) at Dukaladjarranj, an important Dreaming site in Rembarrnga country.

This is my painting of Naworro, spirit ancestor of my clan country who travelled through our land a long time ago. He was a big fella, a big bad spirit man. He had two women. He didn't like them, so he killed them because they annoyed him. He got angry with them on a cliff in the rock country, so he left them in a cave high up in the cliff. They died. That cave is called Kudjekbinj, it is still a very dangerous place. Sometimes we go to that cave and we see his image in the cave, he is in a polished rock, like a coffin.

Roderick Maralngurra

Roderick paints with ochres on bark and paper. He was born in 1971 at the Oenpelli clinic. His language is Kunwinjku, his clan Ngalngbali, his moiety Yirridjdja.

1978

1996

That's me and my younger sister, May, in 1978. We live on different outstations of Ramingining. May Yamangarra is married now, she lives at Nangalala, she has no children. I'm not married, but I have two adopted children, Monica and Alberto. I stay at Yathalamarra in my grandmother's country to look after my parents. I see it's up to me to look after our large family.

Shirley Muyku

Shirley (at left in both photographs) trained as a health worker at Batchelor College near Darwin. May went to college in Queensland and is currently employed at the clinic in Ramingining.

I'm teaching my grandsons about hunting. This is the time for hunting goose eggs. Later everyone will be shooting magpie geese, but now they laying eggs, good time for collecting eggs. This time is season for whistling duck. My brother, George Nawutpu, he's got big mobs of vertigan duck.

David Malangi

David (above) in his mother's country near Yathalamarra, with grandson Daniel. George (opposite) near Galawdjapin.

I worrying for these young people, always playing video, too tired for hunting. When I was young man, my brothers, my cousins and I, we were hunting all the time, hunting with spear, stalking wallaby or goose, fishing barramundi or crocodile. We got so close we could stun six geese with one spear. Now, I'm teaching the young ones, explaining them the seasons, when to hunt turtle, how to follow the track of goanna and wallaby, so they know how to find bush tucker proper Yolngu way.

David Malangi

David's grandson Alberto (opposite) with ibis. Valerie (above) with goanna. The people of eastern and central Arnhem Land call themselves Yolngu, which means 'the people' in Djambarrpuyngu language.

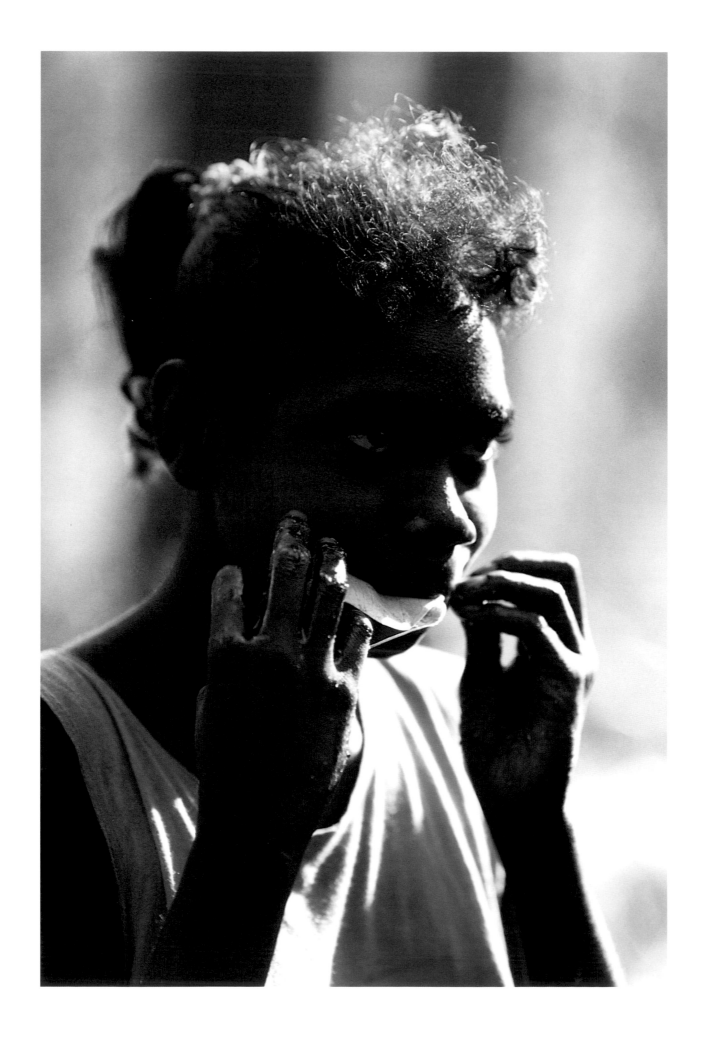

Our grandparents used to teach us about hunting and about our totems. If your totem is ibis, the old law said you must look after ibis, learn everything about ibis, but you mustn't eat your totem. That's what our old people taught us. That way each animal was protected by somebody, that way everybody was looking after their totem. Today people maybe thinking differently.

John Weluk

John's neice Monica (opposite) eating sugarbag. Sugarbag is honey produced by native bees, and can be found in hollow branches or trees. Judy Baypungnala (above) cooking an ibis shot by John, her son.

This is important painting from the Mardayin ceremony. I went through this ceremony when I was a teenager, my father taught me to paint this one. It's about my mother's Dreaming, Dangarrk, in that billabong at Kakodbebuldi. Belongs to the very important secret ceremony, dangerous one. This painting is about Dangarrk, a special plant that makes fire in the water. Very powerful. For initiated men only; if anyone else comes near they will die. The power of that ceremony makes Dangarrk glow in the water. We call that fire barrgarr.

John Mawurndjul

John with his wife, Kay Lindjuwanga, and their children Ananiah and Meniah at Mumeka. John represented Australia at the Biennale in Venice in 1997. He was born in the 1950s at Mumeka. His language is Eastern Kunwinjku, his clan Kurulk, his moiety Yirridjdja.

We come here in the dry season. Now this swamp is drying up, plenty turtle here. Hunting turtle is women's business. Today gathering bush tucker, collecting bush medicine, anything useful and teaching the young girls. Later we cook the turtle, sit around, feel good to be in our country again.

Julie Djulibing

Bush tucker, or bush food, includes (opposite, clockwise from top left): wild gooseberry; cashews; the fruit and seeds of *Tacca leontopetaloides*; cicad nuts, which require several days' leaching to remove toxins before they can be used to make damper (unleavened bread). Julie (above) takes her grandchildren hunting in a paperbark swamp near Mulgurram in Arafura country.

For six months these floodplains
under water, but now it's dry season.
Every day the water drying up, so we
come here to Bulkay, camp beside the
paperbark swamp. Men go hunting
with gun for geese and duck, women
come hunting for turtle. Kids have
good time here, safe from crocodile.

Jill Djalburrburr

The coastal swamps of Arnhem Land, like this
one at Bulkay, are flooded for many months of
the wet season, producing a natural habitat for
wildfowl. As the swamps dry out they become
abundant hunting grounds.

As the water dries up the long-necked turtle hide in the mud. We tread the swamp feeling for the turtle with our feet, tap them with a digging stick for that hollow sound, then pull them out. Later we roast them on the fire. I'm teaching my granddaughter, Monica, teaching the young ones so they learn hunting for themselves.

Judy Baypungnala

A long-necked turtle (opposite) caught at Milmilngkan. Monica and her brother Alberto (above) at Giymir in the Arafura Swamp.

In the wet season that spear grass grows tall, taller than people. But now the grass is drying out, becoming dangerous. This is good time for burning off, for cleaning the country, making it safe. Burning off makes new shoots grow, good too for hunting goanna, snake, wallaby.

Elsie Ganbada

Elsie's granddaughter Monica (above) sets fire to dry grass at Manikapitji. Burning off while the ground is still damp keeps the fire under control and prevents it becoming too hot. Elsie (opposite) with a mundukul, a freshwater python.

We were in school, the wind changed and that bushfire was coming closer and closer, so the teachers said: 'Come on, let's stop that fire!' We pulled some fresh branches and beat the fire back. Everyone had good fun. By the time it was out, there was too much smoke in the classroom to go back to school.

Jessinta and Marion

Children from Ramingining school stamp out the approaching bushfire.

After a burn-off is good time to look for that yellow colour for dyeing pandanus. Plenty hard work getting good colour. First we have to find special yellow root bush. We dig up the root, following that root deep into the ground, cut it off with machete. Later we use it for dyeing pandanus, it makes strong yellow colour. Hard work, but easier to find in clean country.

Clara Matlangadtji

Alena from Kurrurldul (opposite) whose Dreaming is Dangarrk, 'fire in water'. Clara and others from Ramingining (above) return with yellow root wrapped in paperbark. Paperbark can also be used as an instant mat, plate, blanket or umbrella.

Pandanus has razor-sharp barbs and is very tough, you need lots of muscle to pull it. Young girls find it too hard, they have to learn the knack of it. Some old women stronger at pulling pandanus than young ones. When we have plenty of pandanus we take it to a shady spot for splitting while it is still fresh. This is the best part after all the hard work of gathering it. First we strip off the sharp outsides, then bend the soft stem between thumb and finger, push it hard and the fibre splits in two so you can pull it apart, then put it in sun to dry. To make colour, we shave the yellow root with a knife, put the shavings in flour drum and boil with the pandanus. To make red colour we add the ash of ghost gum. For black, we boil gum leaves and special roots. If you mean with colour then you get mean-coloured mat and no one want it!

Fay Matjarra

Women from Ramingining gathering and preparing pandanus at Djakilwirrka. Four species of pandanus are used to make mats and baskets (following pages) that are sold through arts and crafts organisations throughout Australia.

I am traditional owner for this Ganalbingu country near Murwangi in Arafura swamp. Ganalbingu means magpie goose, and I painting this story of my land. Nhulmarmar, my father, taught me to paint when I was a boy. He told me, 'You only paint your own totems, the stories that belong to our family, our ancestors. No one can paint other people's Dreamings.' This painting is about the creation time when the magpie geese flew across this country with a piece of feathered string. They laid that string across the swamp and it became land. We call that place Burgumara.

George Milpurrurru

George's art is held in over a dozen collections in Australia and overseas. A powerful medicine man and important ceremonial leader, he was born in 1936 at Badigalimak, near Mulgurrum. George's language is Ganalbing, his clan Gumang, his moiety Yirritja.

Today everyone want truck. Plenty people got truck now but always worrying for that truck. Everyone taking it, breaking down, fixing it up, always thinking for that truck, too much worry. Sometimes I'm thinking just walking was better. More peaceful.

Oscar Kawurlkku

The number of vehicles – most are 4WD trucks – in Arnhem Land has increased dramatically over the past two decades. Currently, vehicle numbers are said to be doubling every year. Oscar's grandchildren (above, left to right) Isiah, Messiah, Rebecca, Isaaciah and Clancy at Kakodbebuldi outstation. Michael, Jacob and Justin (opposite, left to right) with toy 'wheelie' at Ramingining.

My son Abraham, he's got good eye for buffalo. Abraham, Seymour and those big boys, sometimes they walk all day for buffalo. Maybe they only got five or six bullet so they got to get real close to finish off that buffalo. Many times they come back with nothing, just sore feet, very tired, very hungry; but sometimes they lucky they come back with sore back from carrying all that meat!

Jimmy Njiminjuma

Jimmy's sons and nephews (above, left to right): Abraham Mongkorrerre, Seymour Wulirra, Moses Kurlbakurlba, Kennedy Yiddunu and Adam Wularri at Kakodbebuldi. Moses Kurlbakurlba (opposite) at Kakodbebuldi.

Mimih spirits live in the stone country. They are very shy spirits, they only come out at night or when disturbed. Mimih spirits don't mind people hunting wild creatures, but Mimih spirits are looking after animals that have been tamed, become pets. We tell children if they hurt a pet joey or pet bird that the Mimih spirits will come out after dark and punish them.

Djardie Ashley

A whistling kite (above) is rescued after falling from its nest near Milmilngkan. Djardie's son John (opposite) with a joey at Gilirri.

1978

1997

That was Charlie twenty years ago with all those spears. That shovel-nosed spear was good for getting kangaroo, wild pig and buffalo. Now we got guns for hunting, but that pronged spear still good for fishing. I just got video camera for recording our culture. I'm making video of everything – hunting, gathering, ceremony, basketball, way people living – so we can show the young people in the future.

George Gurralang

Charlie (opposite), now deceased, at Miwirnbi. George (above) with his daughter, Andrea, at Ramingining.

Ramingining is a good place. At school we got lots of computers. Playing on computer is cool, so is basketball and line dancing. We are practising line dancing for fellowship. Fellowship is good for our community, brings everyone together, families, babies, old people sitting together, singing, listening to Bible readings, sometimes sick people are made better.

Teenagers Justin, Andrew, Marion, Noelene and Jacob

Ramingining means 'place of the white cotton', which grew here beside the swamp. The community was founded in the early 1970s, and now has a population of 750, of which one-third have chosen to live on outstations in their own country. Opposite, clockwise from top left: health worker Gladys Wamati at the clinic; studying on the computer in the library; Richard Birrin Birrin playing pool at Nangalala; Andrew Margululu and friends at his outstation, Galawdjapin; the community telephone; Linda Bopirri painting beside her house. Above: Teenagers dancing at Ramingining.

We reckon that kava is good for the community, makes everyone feel happy, makes people sleepy. No more driving to Darwin, having accidents, and fighting. Better too for young people, stopped them petrol sniffing and breaking into houses. Some people spend all their money on kava, but kava is much better than grog, more peaceful.

Charlie Djota

But too many people drinking kava all the time. Young men, drinking all day and all night, never doing anything, just drinking and sleeping. Kava drinkers forget to feed their kids, forget everything. I think kava is killing our culture.

Shirley Muyku

Clinic told me, 'You have to stop drinking kava or you dle'. But when you stop you get sick, really sick, it's too hard. I think the government should do proper research into kava because sometimes we think it's killing our people. We can see what kava is doing to us on the outside, to the skin and sometimes making people have fits, but we worrying about what it's doing to the inside, to the kidneys and to the brain. The government should find out about it.

John Djundurru

Kava (*Piper methysticum*) is a Polynesian shrub. The root is dried and mixed with water to make an intoxicating drink. Kava was introduced in the 1980s by missionaries as a substitute for alcohol.

This one new telephone, this one good story for us. When kids get sick, we telephone clinic, they send truck with medicine. And good for ceremony business too. Every outstation has telephone now, so easy to talk to everyone, make sure everyone turns up for ceremony.

Tom Noytuna

Tom's nephew Mishak (above) fries eggs for breakfast. Tom (opposite) at newly installed phone box at Korlobidahdah.

WATER

Arnhem Land, its people and its history are shaped by water – fresh water and the sea. The warm waters of the Arafura Sea and the Gulf of Carpentaria wash the northern and eastern coasts of Arnhem Land. Inland, rivers snake their way from the sandstone plateaus through rocky gorges and monsoonal forests, releasing their liquid bounty into vast floodplains and tropical swamps. As water is the source of all life, Aboriginal people believe it was created by the ancestral spirits when the world came into being. Water plays an important role in ceremonial life and some waterholes are considered sacred.

Archaeologists and geologists now believe that the original Australians migrated south more than 60,000 years ago, during the last ice age. They are thought to have island-hopped in small rafts from the north. Some 8000 years later, when the earth's climate warmed, the sea rose and forced these first inhabitants further inland. To this day, some coastal people of Arnhem Land still have a relationship with places that are now under the sea, and will avoid certain marine areas that are known to have been important sites during glacial times.

As we climbed aboard a boat at Dhabala, south of Milingimbi Island, David Malangi, elder of the Liyagalawumirri clan, pointed out to sea: 'See there, a hundred metres out? That place, that's Gilimirrgari, special waterhole made by the ancestral spirits, one of the Djangkawu sisters with her digging stick. That

one's fresh water coming up from under the sea, that one belongs to my people.' Certain clans are custodians of these sites that were on land during the ice age, and believe that one day they will return to this submerged land.

Across Arnhem Land, Aboriginal people describe their country through stories and songs recalling the existence and location of the various rivers, wells, billabongs and waterholes. They also ascribe certain powers to their sacred waterholes, some of which are dangerous, others therapeutic and benign.

Until recently people believed that children were conceived by the spirit of their totemic ancestors, an essence of the land that entered a mother's body while she was collecting water. Some months later when the pregnancy became evident, the mother would 'dream' the place and the totem of her child's conception.

This sense of belonging to a set of totemic water-holes is reinforced by ceremonial rites in a person's life, particularly for boys as they pass through the various stages of initiation. When a boy is prepared for circumcision, the designs painted on his chest symbolise his clan's sacred waterholes and the songs associated with them are·sung during his initiation ceremony. At a person's death, male or female, the same songs are sung to transport their spirit back to the land from which it came – a cycle of life that links humankind with nature and eternity.

Long time ago when the world woke up, the Rainbow Serpent, Ngalyod, rose up and made the land and the whale, Mirinyungu, created the ocean. Then the water from the land came rushing down and met the water from the sea. The two great creation creatures, Ngalyod from the land and Mirinyungu from the sea, clashed and caused a big flood. Mirinyungu was superior to the Ngalyod, so the land got covered by sea. The historians and geologists, they know this too, this is true story.

Terry Yumbulul

Boys on the beach at Galiwinku on Elcho Island, off the north-east coast of Arnhem Land.

My paintings represent a reef on the English Companys Islands. The animals were created by the ancestral spirit to look after the reef and one another. This painting is of Octopus and Crayfish, sacred creatures in our ceremony. Only initiated men can dance their dances, women cannot see them.
As I am boss for the Warramiri people, I see my task as protector for this region. I am prepared to argue with government officials and ministers to make them understand that it is important to us Yolngu and to all Australians to protect the life of the sea for the future, for our children and their children's children.

Terry Yumbulul

Several of Terry's commissioned works hang in government buildings in Darwin and Canberra. Terry works closely with the government on both marine and social issues. He was born in 1950 in the Wessel Islands. His language is Warramiri, his clan Warramiri, his moiety Yirritja.

Whale is a prehistoric and sacred animal. My family have been involved with the whale since the beginning of time. The whale is sacred to us Warramiri people, it is our Dreaming. If a whale dies on the beach we make a ceremony for it just like for our people. I'm teaching our children these stories about our great ancestors and all the creatures in the sea. We sing and dance these stories in our ceremonies to celebrate and pass on this knowledge.

Terry Yumbulul

Following a ceremony on the beach the previous night, a group of Warramiri boys spontaneously covered themselves in white clay to show off their knowledge of the mukuy (evil spirits) dance.

We come here in the dry season when the flood plains have dried up, good place for hunting crab, mangrove worms and clams. Aboriginal people been coming here for thousands of years, this beach is all crushed shells, shell midden. The sand is so fine I'm using it to clean my hair. Sometimes we use sand to make crawling babies walk. First we must make a fire under some wet sand, then put that hot sand on the knees and ankles of the baby; gives him strength and helps him walk.

Sylvia Nupunya

Sylvia and her son Dino (above) at Sandy Point on the north coast of Arnhem Land.

This is my father's country. Long time ago in creation time the ancestral spirits, the Djangkawu sisters, made waterholes in this country, some of them are sacred. At Dhabila one of these sweet-water springs comes up in the sea close to the beach. It's a special place for us. When we come here we tell our children these stories so that no one is forgetting.

Shirley Muyku

Shirley's adopted son Alberto (foreground) and Dino paint themselves with mud and play in the shallow sea near Dhabila, while the adults gather mud crabs and other seafood.

1978

1996

That was me and my sisters, Susan and Cheryl, when we were kids. We used to stay here in my mother's country. Dippirri is like an island, you can't get here by land. Now there are six houses here, before we just had bough shelters. They just got new airstrip so the supplies come in by plane. Before in wet season sometimes the boat from Milingimbi [ninety minutes away] couldn't get here. I've come back here by boat with Simeon, my sister Susan's son, to stay with our cousins for a few days, listen to the sea, tell stories, be with my family.

Margie Mutiltja

Margie (opposite, at centre) with Susan and Cheryl at Dippirri, on the north coast of Arnhem Land. Margie and Simeon (above).

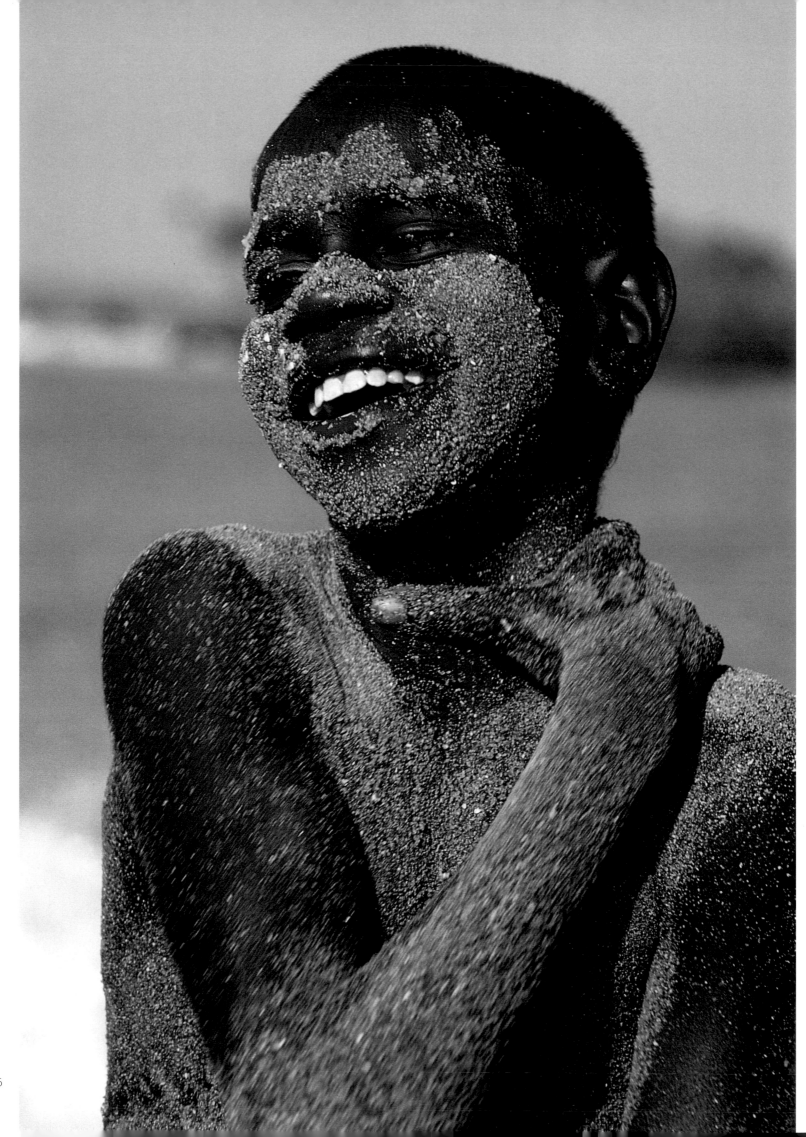

Water is the source of life, fresh water or salt water, water is very important. The sea is like our mother. We are teaching our children about the sea, about their ancestors who came from the sea, to look after the sea and all its creatures and how to fish proper Aboriginal way.

Terry Yumbulul

Ronnie (opposite) and Quentin (above) with a crab caught on the rocks at Dippirri.

Once there was nothing swimming in the sea. Squid found a dark, rocky place to rest. Squid said: 'I'm lonely, I need someone to keep me company.' 'Okay,' said creation spirit, 'there are colourful places on the reef, so I'll send you bright crayfish, he will blend in and hide himself in those colours, and squid with your black ink you can hide in the dark places.' Now I'm teaching the young ones all about the sea creatures, where to find the seafood and how to catch it.

Terry Yumbulul

Amy and Justina (above) at Dippirri with wedu, a sort of catfish. Opposite, clockwise from top left: ritharr, cane grass (a source of water); nonda, longbum or telescopic mud creeper; dhukuray, shellfish; and latjin, mangrove worm.

This painting is kumoken, crocodile, and namarnkol, barramundi, my totems from my clan country, Wardjak near Injalak. Plenty of crocodile in that creek. Kumoken is freshwater crocodile – not dangerous one for humans, just eats barramundi and bream. I'm painting these creatures that live in the creeks and billabongs in my country, and I'm showing the waterlilies and other water plants they feed off.

Simon Badari

Simon paints with ochres on barks and paper. He was born in the 1960s at Oenpelli, and currently lives there. His language is Mayali (Kunwinjku), his clan Wardjak, his moiety Duwa.

This is our grandfather's country, he brings us here sometimes. We catch fish, just walk around, get white clay from billabong, paint ourselves, go looking for things. Our granddad says there are plenty of Mimih spirits here, hiding in rocks. He says white clay keeps away sickness and evil spirits. Now we covered in clay so we can go playing in the rocks and teasing them.

Jeremiah

Jeremiah's brothers Rowen and Matthew (opposite) and sisters (above), using a forked spear to catch fish at Dukaladjarranj.

1978

1996

In Kunwinjku country we have plenty of gapu [fresh water], plenty of rivers, waterholes and springs. This river made by the Rainbow Serpent, Ngalyod, long time ago. I'm showing my children where to find sweet water; warning them about bad and dangerous water. Showing the little ones how to drink so they don't disturb good water. We laugh when we see Balanda [white person] scooping up water with their dirty hands!

Billy Nalakandi

Abraham, Seymour and Ireni (opposite, left to right) drinking from the Mann River. Billy's children (above, left to right) Rayhab, Romeo, Isaac and Susannah at Kabarrebarre in the upper reaches of the same river.

This is my mother's country, Kubumi. There's a special place here where that Rainbow Serpent came up out of the ground at the time of the creation, making all these waterholes in the rock. These waterholes are joined by a creek. We say that this water is the body of the Rainbow Serpent.

Billy Nalakandi

Billy (above) with Rayhab, Romeo and Susannah at Kubumi. Romeo (opposite) at Kubumi.

Djapidijapin is good place for swimming, the water is always cold, very cold. No leeches and crocodiles here, so we can bring our little brothers and sisters. Safe place for picnic, make a fire, cook kangaroo, have fun. We feel this land when we hunting and running around, swimming and having a good time.

Stewart, Andrew and Justin from Ramingining

Left to right: Michelle, Elvin, Jethro and Franko at Djapidijapin, near Ramingining.

Above: Matthew. Below: Gideon (left) and Joshua.

Above: Jerome (left) and Alberto. Below: Gamarrang (left) and Didi.

Below: Lachlan (left) and Brendan.

Below: Roberto.

We always looking for colour, painting up in clay, sand, charcoal is fun. *Jasper*

Kubumi is my mother's country. That mermaid, Yawkyawk, lives in a pool near here. This is my mother's Dreaming. Yawkyawk are spirit creatures. Long time ago they started as tadpoles, but they kept their heads out of the water and developed hair, below the water they grew a fish's tail. Yawkyawk are good spirits. They live in sacred waterholes, they turn into dragonflies, fly around, have adventures, but they always come back to their husbands. We sing them in our ceremonies for being faithful.

Marina Murdilnga

Marina, Billy Nalakandi and their family (above) at Kubumi. Romeo and Susannah (opposite) at Kubumi.

This place is called Mukkamukka after that night bird. Plenty of them in this country. You hear them calling 'muk muk', in the night, and early morning time when you see the morning star. I'm teaching my younger brothers to fish with lure and line.

Seymour Wulirri

Jill Djalburrburr (opposite) fishing at Mukkamukka from a platform. Platforms are also used for sleeping, storing food away from dogs and crocodiles and for laying out the dead. Seymour (above) with his siblings. 'Muk muk' is the call of the tawny frogmouth.

Mukkamukka is my mother's country. When I was young man we stayed here in the dry season. Good place for swimming, fishing, plenty of bush tucker, but too many crocodiles now. Sometimes I paint this country and the Rainbow Serpent that made this place, now I'm painting the crocodile that lives in this billabong. He is very big, very old, a dangerous saltwater crocodile. We call him Kinga.

Jimmy Njiminjuma

Jimmy and family fishing at Mukkamukka.

Long time ago the crocodile ancestor was important man. He lived in the bush. He wanted to go beyond the mountains he could see in the distance but the escarpment was too steep to climb, so he turned into a crocodile and swam upriver. He gnawed his way through the mountain and created the Liverpool River. Every year he brings his mate back upstream from the sea to lay her eggs in the fresh water.

Thompson Yulidjirri

Too many crocodile in my country! So now I'm working in new crocodile business at Muwangi. Crocodile is totem for me. I know everything about crocodile, so I'm showing Balanda how to get those crocodile eggs just at right time, just before the baby crocs break out. Dangerous work, pays five dollars per egg. We put the eggs in a special incubator, and when they hatched we fly them to crocodile farm in Darwin.

George Milpurrurru

Aboriginal rock artists have depicted freshwater crocodiles for 50,000 years. Saltwater crocodiles first appear in rock art about 8000 years ago.

1978

1996

That's me in 1978, wearing waterlily for decoration, for fun. Now I showing my daughter Darolyn same way. Waterlilies are part of our Dreaming, good tucker too. Waterlilies grow all year round. We can eat every bit of them, flower, stem and corm. When we ran out of flour sometimes my mother made damper from that corm.

David Warapuwuy

Dhulumburrk, waterlilies, are abundant throughout Arnhem Land, especially in paperbark swamps and billabongs.

This painting is about that dingo dog Adjumarllarl. He travelled through this country long time ago with the female dog Walbulbul. She only had three legs. They came to this place looking for water, but the female dog couldn't climb the cliff, so Adjumarllarl left her behind. He climbed the cliff, dug into the rock and made the waterfall. When he returned the female dingo had turned into a rock, that three-legged rock near here. I paint this story and I am explaining to my son this place of my Dreaming so he knows this story, will tell his family, keep our Dreaming alive for future generations.

Tony Bangalang

Tony paints with ochres on bark and paper, and his work hangs in the Department of Foreign Affairs building in Canberra. Tony was born in 1959 in Darwin, and now lives on the outstation at Mikinj Valley. His language is Kunwinjku, his clan Murrawan, his moiety Yirridjdja.

SPIRIT

The great creation ancestors, the totemic spirits, brought light into the darkness and created the world as it is today. The exploits of these ancestral beings – whether Ngalyod the Rainbow Serpent, Mirinyungu the whale or Baru the crocodile – are symbols of spiritual and historical significance to the people for whom they are totems.

For many people in Arnhem Land, this belief in the creation spirits found common ground with the concept of God the creator and the principles of Christianity. In embracing Christian faith, Aboriginal people see no conflict in singing Christian hymns, while at the same time participating in ceremonies to uphold their totemic beliefs and kinship system.

Good spirits and evil spirits are part of everyday life, as Shirley Muyku, one of the health workers at Ramingining, explained: 'The spirit creatures made this land, made our law, made everything, and some of them hang around to remind us where we came from; to remind us to look after our land and its creatures, as well as the law. Most people I know are superstitious; they will never walk around alone at night for fear of all the spirits.'

In western Arnhem Land the rocky escarpment country is said to be the home of the shy nocturnal Mimih spirits. Paintings attributed to the Mimih are found in caves and remote rock shelters. 'Some of those spirits are very cheeky, they can be dangerous without really meaning to be, make people scared,'

explained artist Thompson Yulidjirri as we inspected the fine figures painted high up in one of the caves near Injalak. People also believe the Marrkidjbu, or medicine men, are able to communicate with the Mimih spirits and incite them to cast spells on people in revenge or for punishment.

Magic and sorcery are also linked with the spirits through myth and ritual. For example, red ochre is said to have the power to heal and protect, while white clay is used to cleanse or invoke fear. Painting with ochres is used not only to educate or illustrate the important myths but also to decorate sacred artifacts, significant regalia, totemic barks, religious icons and hollow-log coffins. Body painting is an integral part of the ritual of ceremony for which sacred objects are prepared, and the ceremonial sites can have special or secret significance.

When a person dies, although the cause of death can be explained in terms of Western medicine, an evil spirit or sorcerer is often blamed. The women perform cleansing ceremonies that involve burning special leaves to smoke out the dangerous spirits, or a medicine man evokes good spirits to drive the evil ones away. Throughout Arnhem Land the elaborate mortuary rites of different clans vary, however their purpose is the same. Relatives of a deceased person gather for a final ceremonial ritual to ensure that the deceased's spirit returns to its place of origin, the land of the totemic spirits from which it came.

This is ngangiyal, a special tent made of woven pandanus. It is used for women's business. In old times when a young girl got her first period they put her inside the tent, away from the camp. The old women looked after her till it was over. Today we are going to use the tent in a healing ceremony. Elsie has big problems in her back and chest, she can't breathe properly, so we have brought her back to Manikapitji, her country, to make her better.

Judy Baypungnala

Judy's grandchildren play with the ngangiyal on the mud flats at Manikapitji, south of Milingimbi.

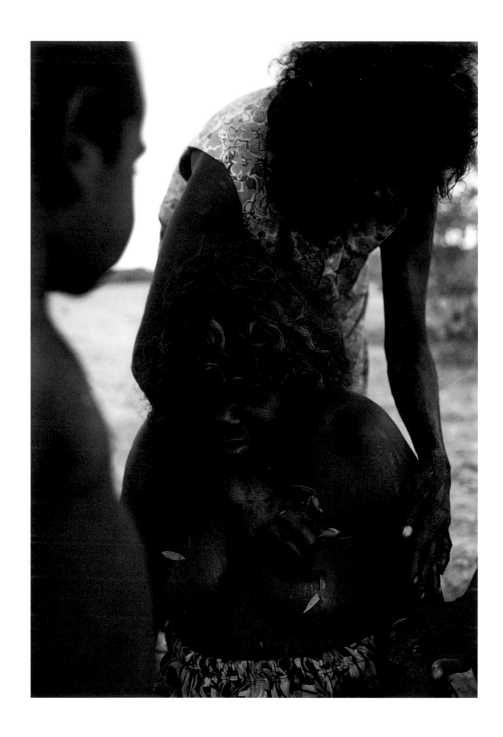

Elsie Ganbada's totem is possum. Possum droppings are what we need to help her. If we can't find them we use white clay to represent the possum droppings. When it is rubbed into Elsie's skin it starts healing and will make her strong. For this healing we use rangan, the young leaves from the paperbark tree. Baypungnala strips the leaves from the branch and crushes them in water for inhaling and rubbing. As Elsie breathes through the crushed leaves she feels the essence of the paperbark clearing inside of her.

Shirley Muyku

Shirley's mother Elsie (above) being treated by her co-wife Judy Baypungnala. Elsie (opposite) inhaling the leaves.

We have come here, away from all the noise of the camp, so that this healing process will give Elsie strength and make her better. The women and girls are joining in to make a ceremony round Elsie. All of us singing and rubbing and dancing with paperbark leaves, trying to make Elsie better. Elsie is covering herself with white clay to get rid of that sickness while she sleeps on the paperbark in the traditional woven tent. I watched my grandmother doing this healing, she taught me this traditional Yolngu way.

Shirley Muyku

Shirley is knowledgeable in Yolngu medicine and is also a trained health worker. The healing ceremony started in the afternoon and by next morning Elsie was feeling better.

Through ceremony we pass on our law, we sing and dance the stories of our ancestors, our totemic heroes, so this knowledge will last forever. Some ceremonies are secret–sacred for initiated men only, last for months. Other ceremonies with women and young people too, public bunggul. All the time we taking ceremony, this way, that way, teaching the young people all the time, teaching them Yolngu law, about our culture through ceremony business.

George Milpurrurru

The feathered string in this bunggul represents a story of Barnumbirr the Morning Star, which carries the souls of some deceased people back to a land beyond the sunrise.

1979

144

1997

That's us at our dhapi, our initiation ceremony, at Nangalala. We were young boys then. We are all still here, sometimes hunting, working on outstation, making garden, planting fruit trees, playing cards, drinking kava and sometimes making ceremony. Today's initiates call us old men!

Ralph Baymonunbi

Above, clockwise from left: Steve Djunanu, Bruce Bulun Bulun, Robert Madawali and Ralph Baymonunbi. Opposite, from left: Steve, Robert, Ralph and Bruce.

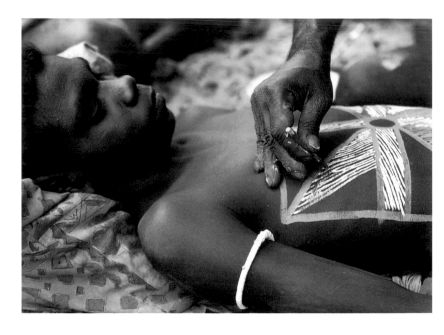

This is my son Jazmin's dhapi. I am painting on his chest that sacred waterhole Milmildjarrk near Dhamala. It was made by one of the Djangkawu sisters with her digging stick. The Djangkawu sisters travelled through this land creating the clans and giving us our languages. They named the places, the sacred waterholes, and gave the different clans the law. This story I'm painting belongs to my father David Malangi. We are custodians for this story about our people, we sing and dance this story in our ceremonies. This is my father's story which he gave to me and I am giving it to my son.

Richard Birrin Birrin

Opposite, clockwise from top left: an elder wearing a sacred dilly bag; Jazmin being prepared by the men for his initiation at Yathalamarra; Jazmin before his circumcision (also above); Peter, Solomon and Daniel during their initiation.

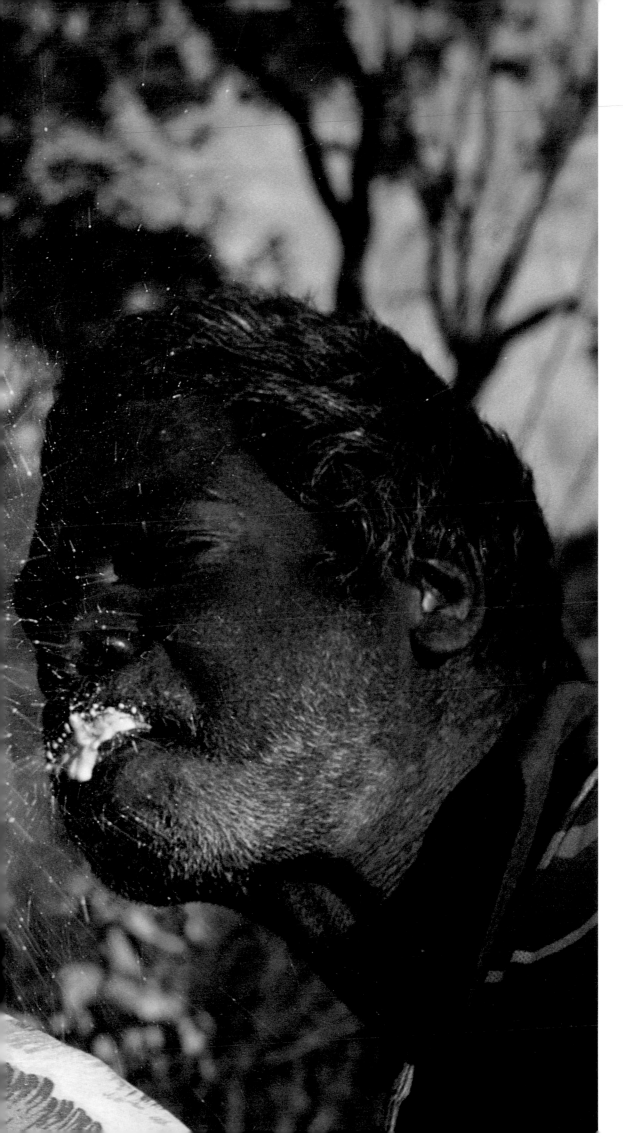

Jazmin, my son, is old enough now to start learning our law, he is thirteen. All our boys go through initiation ceremony to make them men, then later when they are older we put them through secret–sacred men's ceremony. Jazmin's dhapi, his initiation, is his first step into our sacred law. After this he will join the other men in men's business. This is the traditional way for ceremony. We cover ourselves with white clay and red ochre to show our children how to keep the law and keep our culture strong. When the Djangkawu sisters travelled across the land they carried a sacred dilly bag made of orange parrot feathers and white ibis down. In that bag they kept the sacred objects and their special tools. Today Jazmin will wear this bag and sacred armbands: these emblems have a special meaning for us.

Richard Birrin Birrin

Jazmin's face is spray painted with white pipe-clay by his uncle David Datpurkarri. Following pages: applying white clay, gamunuggu (left), and sacred armbands of parakeet feathers and ibis down (right), for ceremony.

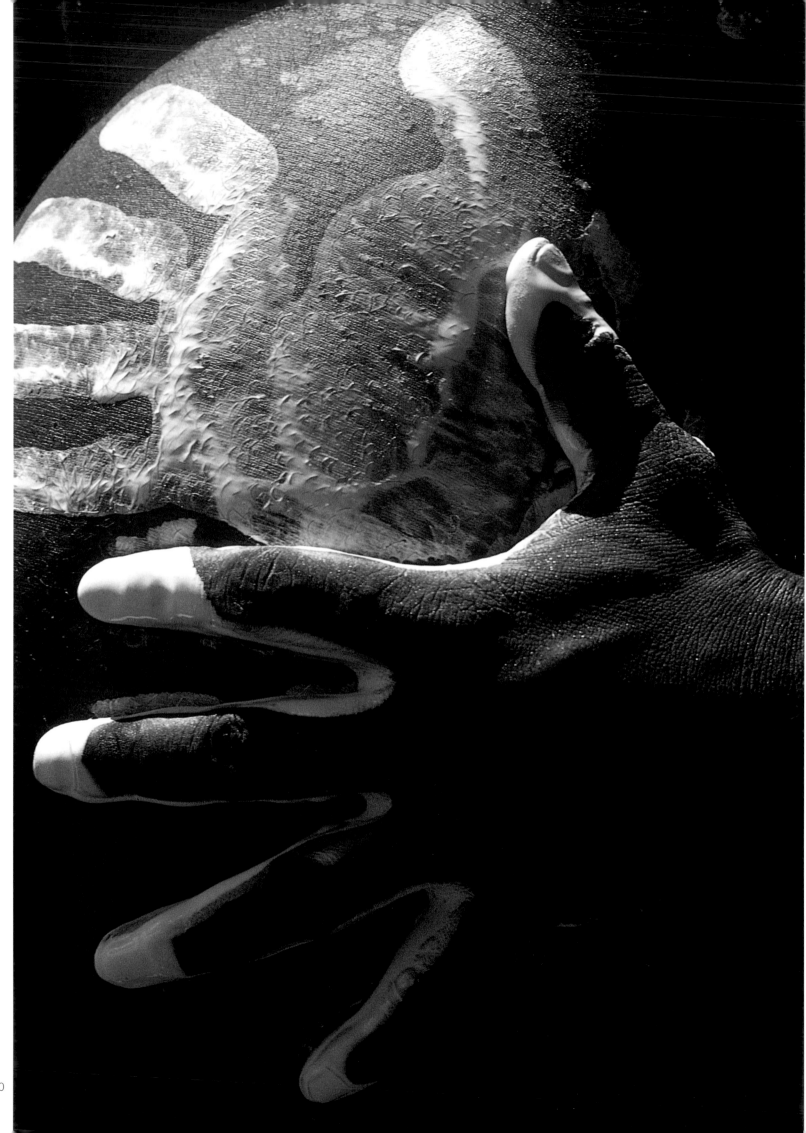

1979

1996

That was a dhapi at Nangalala in 1979. We were bringing the young initiates into the ceremony ground to watch the dancing. Today we are bringing my nephew Jazmin to be initiated here at Yathalamarra. We cover Jazmin's head as we bring him into the ceremony ground for his circumcision. We make this ceremony for him to make him man. This is our traditional way.

John Costa

Jazmin's father Richard, his uncles John and David and many of the others (above) were among the participants at the Nangalala dhapi (opposite) in 1979.

I am happy for my nephew, he is young man now. Jazmin will go through many ceremonies in his life, learning more and more about our sacred law. We are teaching our young men so there will always be custodians to keep this law strong.

John Costa

John (opposite) and his granddaughter watch Jazmin (above) being carried away after his circumcision. During the ceremony and the days that followed Jazmin was cared for by his cousin Troy.

I am painting since I was boy, painting my country, my totems, painting my special waterhole, Milmildjarrk, that one made by the Djangkawu sisters with their digging stick. We sing and dance Milmildjarrk in our ceremonies. And I paint the story of Gurrumurringu the great hunter. That one they call 'dollar note' painting because it was printed on the one-dollar note. It shows the mortuary rites for the great hunter, Gurrumurringu, who was killed by Dharpa, the evil snake.

David Malangi

David with some of his paintings at Bula Bula, Ramingining. Milmildjarrk is represented in the paintings to the left and right of him. David was awarded an honorary Doctorate of Laws by the Australian National University in 1996 for his 'distinguished creative contribution in the service of society'. David was born in 1927 at Muliyanga. His language is Djinang, his clan Liyagalawumirri subsection Manyarrngu, his moiety Dhuwa.

Milmildjarrk is my father Malangi's sacred waterhole, his Dreaming. Same one that was painted on Jazmin for his dhapi. It is fresh water in middle of saltwater floodplain. My father is traditional owner for this sacred place, but he is very sick. My sister Shirley and I, we are coming here to get this special water for our father to give him strength.

May Yamangarra

May drawing water at Milmildjarrk.

Malangi is my ngapippi, my uncle. He is the traditional elder for us Manyarrngu people, but he is sick, too much sorry business, always worrying for the future of our family. Now everyone worrying for him. Malangi came in essence from this water, Milmildjarrk. His daughters, Shirley and May, are getting this special water to help him. Malangi must drink this water, bathe in this water, to keep him strong.

Joan Djikanmurruwuy

Joan (opposite). May and Shirley (above), with Malangi's grandson Alberto, returning from Milmildjarrk with the sacred water.

David Rumba Rumba

Elizabeth Lilipyana

Rosie Wudam

Terry Yumbulul

Brian Campion

Jackie Bungannyal

George Milpurrurru

David Malangi

Thompson Yulidjirri and Mark

We call this place Dirdbim, place of the Moon Dreaming. Since long ago we bury our old people in the cave here. I bring my children here to tell them the story for this place. Long time ago the spotted quoll lived here to guard this burial site. One day the Rainbow Serpent, Ngalyod, pierced the rock in the back of the cave and placed the Moon Dreaming at Dirdbim. The quoll was upset by this intrusion. So the quoll and the moon had a big argument about the fate of humanity. The moon said that people should be able to live forever. The quoll said that if everyone was allowed to live forever, there would be too many people and there wouldn't be enough food for everyone. To prove his point the quoll fell down dead. But the moon said: 'I'm buggered if I am going to die forever. I'll just go up into the sky and disappear, then I'll come back again.' So every month the moon dies, but is reborn a few days later to remind everyone of his power.

Billy Nalakandi

Billy (above) with his children at Dirdbim. Billy shows Romeo (opposite) the place of the Moon Dreaming.

We are telling our children the stories
so they not forgetting. Our children
will tell their children so that our
history, our culture, will go on and
on forever. This is our Aboriginal way.

Jacob Nayinggul

Jacob's nephews Rowen, Brian and Thomas making
music as the sun goes down.

BIBLIOGRAPHY

Aboriginal Land Rights Commission, Parliamentary Paper No. 138 (Woodward Reports), Government Printer, Canberra, 1973, 1974.

Barwick, Diane, *Aboriginal and Islander History*, Australian National University Press, Canberra, 1979.

Bell, D. R., *Daughters of the Dreaming*, McFee Gribble, Melbourne, 1983.

Bell, D., and Ditton, P., *Law: The Old and New*, Australian National University Press, Canberra, 1980.

Berndt, C. H. and R. M., *Pioneers and Settlers*, Pittman, Melbourne, 1978.

Berndt, R. M. and C. H., *The First Australians*, Ure Smith, Sydney, 1952.

— *The World of the First Australians*, Ure Smith, Sydney, 1964.

— *Love Songs of Arnhem Land*, Nelson, Melbourne, 1978.

— *Arnhem Land: Its History and Its People*, Cheshire, Melbourne, 1954.

Caruana, Wally, and Lendon, Nigel, *The Paintings of the Wagilag Sisters Story, 1937–1997*, National Gallery of Australia, Canberra, 1997.

Chaloupka, George, *Journey in Time*, Reed, Sydney, 1993.

Cole, Keith, *The Aborigines of Arnhem Land*, Rigby, Sydney, 1993.

Donaldson, Ian and Tamsin (eds), *Seeing the First Australians*, Allen and Unwin, Sydney, 1985.

Elkin, A. P., *Aboriginal Men of High Degree*, 2nd ed, University of Queensland Press, St Lucia, 1977 (first publ. 1946).

— *The Australian Aborigines*, Angus and Robertson, Sydney, 1974.

Gale, Fay (ed) *Women's Role in Aboriginal Society*, Australian Institute of Aboriginal Studies, Canberra, 1974.

Groger-Wurm, Helen M., *Australian Aboriginal Bark Painting in North-East Arnhem Land*, Australian Institute of Aboriginal Studies, Canberra, 1973.

Hughes, Robert, *The Fatal Shore*, Collins Harvill, London, 1987.

Isaacs, Jenny, *Australian Dreaming*, Lansdowne, Sydney, 1980.

Kluge, John W. (ed), *Kunwinjku Art from Injalak 1991–92*, Museum Art International, Adelaide, 1994.

McKenzie, Maisie, *Mission to Arnhem Land*, Rigby, Adelaide, 1976.

Mountford, C. P., *Art, Myth and Symbolism of Australian Aborigines in Arnhem Land*, Melbourne University Press, Melbourne, 1956.

National Gallery of Australia, *The Art of George Milpurrurru*, Canberra, 1993.

Poignant, Alex and Roslyn, *Encounter at Nagalarramba*, National Library of Australia, Canberra, 1996.

Powell, Alan, *Far Country: A Short History of the Northern Territory*, Melbourne University Press, Melbourne, 1982.

Ranger Uranium Environmental Inquiry, First Report (Fox Report), AGPS, Canberra, 1976.

Robert, W. C. H., *The Dutch Explorers of Australia 1605–1756*, Philo Press, Amsterdam, 1973.

Roberts, J., *From Massacres to Mining: The Colonisation of Aboriginal Australia*, CIMRA, London, 1978.

Rowley, C. D., *Outcasts in White Australia*, Australian National University Press, Canberra, 1971.

— *Remote Aborigines*, Australian National University Press, Canberra, 1971.

— *The Destruction of Aboriginal Society*, Australian National University Press, Canberra, 1970.

Searcy, A., *In Northern Seas*, W. K. Thomas, Adelaide, 1905.

Shapiro, W., *Social Organisation in Aboriginal Australia*, Australian National University Press, Canberra, 1979.

Spencer, Sir W. Baldwin, *Preliminary Report on the Aboriginals of the Northern Territory*, Melbourne, 1913.

Stone, S. (ed), *Aborigines in White Australia*, Heinemann, Melbourne, 1974.

Tatz, C., *Race Politics in Australia*, University of New England Publications Unit, Armidale, 1979.

Thomson, Donald, *Report on Expedition to Arnhem Land 1936–37*, Canberra, 1939.

Tweedie, Penny, *This My Country*, Collins, Sydney, 1985.

Warner, W. L., *A Black Civilisation*, Harper and Row, New York, 1958.

Williams, Nancy N., *The Yolngu and Their Land*, Australian Institute of Aboriginal Studies, Canberra, 1986.

Published in the UK in 1998 by
New Holland Publishers (UK) Ltd
London • Sydney • Auckland • Cape Town
24 Nutford Place London W1H 6DQ United Kingdom
14 Aquatic Drive Frenchs Forest NSW 2086 Australia
1A/218 Lake Road Northcote Auckland New Zealand
80 McKenzie Street Cape Town 8001 South Africa

Produced in Australia in 1998 by
New Holland Publishers (Australia) Pty Ltd

Copyright © 1998 Penny Tweedie
Copyright © 1998 photographs Penny Tweedie
Copyright © 1998 pages 18–23 text George Chaloupka
Copyright © 1998 map New Holland Publishers (Australia) Pty Ltd
Copyright © 1998 New Holland Publishers (Australia) Pty Ltd

All rights reserved. No part of this publication may be reproduced, stored in a retrieval system or transmitted, in any form or by any means, electronic, mechanical, photocopying, recording or otherwise, without the prior written permission of the publishers and copyright holders.

National Library of Australia Cataloguing-in-Publication Data:

Tweedie, Penny, 1940- .
Aboriginal Australians: spirit of Arnhem Land.

ISBN 1 86436 330 4.

1. Aborigines, Australian - Northern Territory - Arnhem Land - Social life and customs. 2. Aborigines, Australian - Northern Territory - Arnhem Land - Pictorial works. I. Title.

994.2950049915

Publishing General Manager: Jane Hazell
Publisher: Averill Chase
Project Manager: Narelle Walford
Designer: Patricia McCallum
Editor: Kerry Davies
Editorial Consultants: Ian Connellan, Howard Whelan
Design Consultant: Tony Gordon
Map Illustrator: Marje Crosby-Fairall
Reproduction: Colour Symphony
Printer: Tien Wah Press, Singapore

Penny Tweedie thanks: